Praise

"With so many self-styled experts issuing proclamations about education, it's high enough time to learn the views and recommendations of a thoughtful young person."
-Alan Kay, Turing Award Recipient, President of the Viewpoints Research Institute

"A passionate, outspoken teenager tells us how to improve education based on his own experiences and frustrations and his interviews with an array of experts."
-Guido van Rossum, Creator of the Python Programming Language, Dropbox Employee

"Aaron, at a very early age, is already a contributor to our society. I'm sure this book is only the first of many to come from him."
-Dr. Robert Marzano, Founder of Marzano Research, Experienced Author and Speaker of Education Reform

"Education today faces three emerging and singular conditions. We are preparing a genuinely unique generation of children, within a significantly new digital information environment, for a future that we can no longer clearly describe. It is certainly time that educators combine the best of pedagogical research and our deeply held values, with the voices, experiences and ideas of students, who are entering our classrooms wired to learn."
-David Warlick, Retired Itinerant Educator, Author, Programmer, 2011 Technology & Learning Magazine "Top Ten Most Influential People in EdTech" Recipient

What Middle School Didn't Teach Me

Aaron J. Lafazan

What Middle School Didn't Teach Me

Aaron J. Lafazan

AUSTIN ∎ DALLAS ∎ NEW YORK ∎ PHILADELPHIA ∎ SAN FRANCISCO

Published in the United States by Next Gen Publishing, a division of Next Gen Ventures, New York
www.NextGenSummit.us
Next Gen Publishing is a trademark of Next Gen Ventures, Inc.

What Middle School Didn't Teach Me is a trademark of Aaron Lafazan and used under license

Next Gen Publishing
PermissionCoordinator@NextGenPublishing.org
SpecialSalesDepartment@NextGenPublishing.org
Team@NextGenPublishing.org
www.NextGenPublishing.org

Printed in the United States of America

Ordering Information: Special Discounts are available on quantity purchases by corporations, associations, and other. For details, contact the 'Special Sales Department' at the address above.

Book Cover ©2015 GFB, Inc.
Book Layout ©2013 BookDesignTemplates.com

What Middle School Didn't Teach Me / Aaron Lafazan —1st ed.

ISBN-13: 978-0692592137 (Next Gen Publishing)
ISBN-10: 069259213X
Library of Congress Control Number: 2015921423

Contents

To The Fantastic Four: Mom, Dad, Josh, and Justin
If It Weren't For You, I'd Be Watching Netflix Right Now

Acknowledgements

Wow. I never really thought I would get this far! Honestly, I always thought that this book would become one of those side hobbies that you throw away after facing too much hardship, too much failure. It got close. But, at the end of the day, I didn't throw it away, and that's all that counts.

The people I have to thank for that: My fantastic, ferocious, funny, friendly, frantic, faultless, flourishing, and fascinating family, whom I love with every fiber of my being (even when nobody admits I'm the best basketball player in the house). My friends, who've helped me keep going (especially with the help of Noice Vibes), and allowed me to continue having a social life during the creation of this book. And, last but not least, to the people who have probably helped me most: everyone who hated on me and who ripped on me for trying to do something different. Seriously, thanks. They were the reason why at 3 AM on a Sunday, I would go to write rather than to go to sleep (or get McDonalds Ice Cream Cones with my brothers).

Finally, I am so thankful that I was born into a life where I am able to get everything I need, from support in times of need to the resources at my disposal, which put me in the best place to succeed.

Education is the most powerful weapon which you can use to change the world.

—Nelson Mandela

Preface

Education. It's kind of a big deal. Yet I feel most people seriously undervalue it. I think in society today, education should be seen as something with greater importance.

When I think of domestic issues, the major problems that seem to spring to mind include the economy, politics, and then education. It is my belief that education is so greatly important in our society; in my mind, if we want to make America the best it can be, we need proper education for our future success. I believe the 'chain of success' would start students with great educations, so that our number of successful people continues to multiply.

With that said, policymakers, administrators, teachers, and all others in these types of positions in education need to understand one thing: today's Middle School education is essentially the equivalent of a Horror Story. Not only is our education bland, but also it is rather a letdown if students want to make a name for ourselves in the world.

Countless times I see the same issues, where multitudes of kids are unable to go about or succeed at very menial tasks that should've been taught in middle schools. For me, this is everything from public speaking to understanding how our economy works; things that I believe everyone should be able to know.

In this book, I've thought personally about a handful of different topics that middle school didn't teach me, and how they could have been improved to put me in the best position to succeed in life. These are both skills and subjects that I feel time could have been utilized effectively for the overall betterment of the student. These are:

➤ Mathematics
➤ Computer Science
➤ Financial Literacy
➤ Communication Skills
➤ Language
➤ Logic
➤ Public Speaking
➤ Writing

In addition, towards the end of the book, you'll find a few student pieces reflecting on their own thoughts on middle school education, as well as 'Final Thoughts On Education' pieces from true educational experts.

Overall, I've tried to make sure my approach in creating change was backed for from all angles and experiences, to ensure that what I am saying is *right* (or at least to some degree). I have a collection of experience in education ranging from students to teachers to administration to professionals in their respective fields.

Now, before I go on, I must warn you: Many call this book, or at least the idea of the book, a rant. Yes, this is true to some degree. I do get angry at middle schools, simply because of the disadvantages for which my peers and I have to deal with daily. I just think that there is so much potential for success with middle school, and I tend to get angry when I look back and realize all of that potential was wasted. So, is this book a rant? A little bit. But mostly, it's the written opinions and beliefs of many others around me and myself, in a somewhat relaxed manner (or at least more so than the original finished product).

In totality, my philosophy about middle school can be summed up in a simple one liner: teach what you need to teach, and give students the stepping-stones of the important parts of life.

For the first part of that saying, teaching *what needs to be taught*, it is my philosophy that middle school of all places should just teach you the important stuff. The fact that there continues to be double periods of science throughout the years in middle school is despicable, when they could instead take that period and transform it into programs such as my future idea of a 'revolving business period', which you'll read more about later. So, we need to change what we teach, to teach what's important and make sure that our students can't come out of middle school with disadvantages from lack of good content.

Bjarne Stroustrup says it best, in that, when asked his thoughts on education as a whole, "I think being able to think rationally is key, to avoid fooling yourself with faulty logic and unreliable 'facts.' To do that you need a base of knowledge to build on: history (of more than one country and era), litera-ture (preferably varied and including a fair bit of classical ma-terial), science (physics, chemistry, biology), math (including some probability and statistics), at least one foreign language (learned well, to understand a foreign culture), some sociolo-gy/civics to see how societies function, possibly a bit of engi-neering (to see how science is put to use). The ability to organize and present material (verbally and in writing). Some of this is done everywhere, but emphasis differs dramatically, as does the depth of engagement with the material. Obviously, this is a whole lot of material, but I'm thinking of a complete education: kindergarten to University."

Now, onto the second part, *giving us the stepping-stones.* I believe that middle school students, overall, can't handle in-depth analysis of subjects. It's not that kids at this age can't be smart, I just believe, from personal experiences, middle school kids have not developed enough brain capacity or experience in analysis to succeed in an in-depth study in every subject. This is why for everything I propose, I believe that only the basics should be taught. If a foundation of important topics were taught, than these could be expanded on later, with stu-dents then having the ability to succeed in their endeavors pertaining to that subject.

With that said, when I would tell people about the fact that I am writing a book about middle schools, most of them just laugh. Most people think it's unimportant. Most think there is no point in dedicating time to something as silly as education reform in middle schools. They'll say, "Aaron, why don't you just write *What Preschool Didn't Teach Me?*'" For every expert interview I was able to get (thanks to those who said yes), I've had a dozen adults laugh at my proposals. I had to send out over 2,000 emails to adults I wanted to interview for 20 incredible experts to agree. For every one kid my own age who thought that what I was doing was cool, I've had so many laugh in my face, telling me I shouldn't be wasting my time on something so unimportant like middle schools. For a while, I thought this as well. I thought middle school was a joke, and shouldn't need to be changed.

However, once I started to really think about it, and notice everything going on around me, small things that easily could've been fixed, I realize that middle school should in fact be a priority.

This is for countless reasons, but I'll give you my top argument:

Simply put, it's because Middle School is the stepping-stone for high school, and the rest of your life. Elementary school is something that shouldn't be worried about, because at this age, nose picking is more important than good grades. But middle school prepares you for high school, which is arguably the first real stepping stone into advanced education, and beyond; as such, we need to prepare students for that big first leap in education.

Everything you learn in middle school translates into what the basics of what you know for the rest of your life. That's why it's so important that we provide all students the foundations for this learning. It's not because what they learn in middle school will span all of their knowledge as it relates to that specific topic. Rather, it's meant to give students the basics of what they need to succeed. In my opinion at least, it's so much easier to build up than to start new. After all, most often, is it easier to start building a new house from scratch, or to build on an older house's foundation?

Think about when you learn something new. Do you get thrown all the information that you'll ever need on that one topic in 2 seconds? No. First, you get the basics, what you need to build up. Then, you expand.

Now, for a little bit about me, as you're probably asking, 'who is this kid to write a book about education reform?'

My name is Aaron Lafazan, and I've been excelling since I could walk. I was raised in a household where good was never good enough; where unless you were doing well, unless you were succeeding, you were doing it all wrong. Tough in a good way parents and brothers who pushed me constantly showed me how success could be attained if you worked for it, and I strove to achieve it early on.

Currently, I am a sophomore in high school, maintaining a 98.5 average, participating in numerous extra-curricular activities in my town, and I am starting an event destined to change computer science on the east coast. I'm also a computer science nut in general. As you'll read throughout the book, I've started to develop an incredibly passionate feeling towards computers and computer programming, a skill that I think everyone should have, especially as a foundation to have in middle schools across the country. Oh, and there's one more thing, that I always forget: I'm a 15 year old published author, who has put in too many hours to count in an effort to break a story he feels is incredibly important, someone who isn't afraid to put his thoughts out there for everyone to read. I'm someone who is willing to participate in change.

Now, my intentions for this book are very simple:

1.   To make sure everyone who has the attention span to read a book understands the problems in middle school education today

2.   To make every middle school curriculum top of the line and 21st century based.

On that note of my intentions for the book, I would like to point out one thing. This book mainly is focused around New York State middle school curriculum, considering that many of my classmates and I go to school there. However, the concepts addressed in this book apply to everyone, so regardless of where you live, keep on reading. Bjarne Stroustrup says it best: "Young people are taught very different things in different places. It would be a mistake to think that everyone – even everyone in one US city – was taught the same in the same way." Stroustrup is not an expert in education, but rather is an expert computer programmer, one who has much experience in both programming itself as well as teaching programming (he heavily teaches computer science at Texas A&M University).

Overall, it is almost impossible to believe that my book can affect every part of the US – each state has their own way of doing it. All in all, this book *targets* New York State Curriculum makers, but the concepts in this book are very general, and apply to any and every other part of the world.

Where The Book Came From

This book is my baby. As such, I'll share the details of its conception.

The real *motivation* to actually write a book came a little before the creation of the book idea itself.

It was a regular Friday night, and my family and I were out for our weekly family dinner. My brother Justin was set to fly to Las Vegas the following morning for a talk, and began to share an idea that was brewing in his head: writing a book about how young people can design the lives they want to live. My other brother Josh perked up, as Justin's concept resonated with him; having become New York State's youngest elected official in 2012, Josh believed that, with the right collection of experts, he as well could educate and inspire on his subject area of running for office, and so Josh quickly joined Justin in the writing process. My two older brothers were set to write their respective books and launch them together, in a "Two Brothers Book Launch."

Then I was all alone, by myself. One of the biggest things you'll need to know about me is that I hate coming in last, and that I hate being the one left out. Well, that was the motivation to write a book. I didn't care at the time that I was 14 when my brothers were already legal adults, and that my brothers had to think about college when I had to think about what was for dinner. I didn't care. I always fight my brothers to do everything earlier than them, to try to be better than them, so it didn't matter.

Fast-forward another month. My brother Justin and I were engaging in one of our common routines: we were on our way to go grabs some delicious Vanilla ice-cream cones from McDonalds in his Honda Civic, at about 3 o'clock in the morning, listening to the song "Hold On, We're Going Home" by the famous philosopher Aubrey Graham, better known as the rapper Drake. On our way, I was talking to him about school, and about my friends who lacked in things like public speaking, and how even I myself was behind in many aspects of school. Ones that easily could've been fixed. And then I said those faithful words: 'I wish I would've learned it in middle school.'

Immediately, gears turned in Justin's head. He then asked me, 'Aaron, what if you write a book about middle school education reform?' A question that would change my life forever.

My initial thought, though, was 'Hell no!' It was because at the time, I was one of those people who didn't think middle school was important.

But then, after much prodding from him and a little bit of soul searching, I realized how great of an idea it was, and that I would need to get the ball rolling as soon as possible to make change. I knew one thing: I needed to make middle schools across this country more practical, which would require serious change. That was my goal when I first started, and that still is my goal today.

That's when Two Became Three.

And that's one thing I'll forever be grateful for: my family always looking out for me, trying to do what's best for me, and to lead me in the right direction.

With the Three Brothers Book Launch, we were then able to approach Next Gen Publishing, and after given the go-ahead with their backing, our dreams became realities: the Lafazan Brothers, at 15, 19, and 21 would conquer the world and publish their books TOGETHER!

Final Remarks

For more about me, feel free to check me out at aaronlafazan.com, or shoot me an email at aaron@aaronlafazan.com. I'd be happy to answer any and every question.

Finally, for helping me get through my struggles and my difficulties, especially with this 'monster' I call my book, I would like to commend a few people who I feel deserve a place in my special piece of art yet another time.

To my beautiful parents: Mom and Dad, I know at times I can get really annoying and hurtful, but thanks for loving me anyway. Thanks for everything you do, and for guiding me in the right direction, and always giving me the possibility of success. Love you both.

To my brothers Josh and Justin: Boys, what's there really to say? You guys know you're my best friends for life, and that I'll never stop loving you both till the day I die. I love you guys, and thank you for always looking out for me, for caring for me, for pushing me, for saying what needed to be said as opposed to what I wanted to hear.

And to my other 'bros', my friends: Thanks so much you guys. You're the reason I got this done. Love you guys, and you're the best friends anyone could ask for.

With my acknowledgments given, go on and explore the rest of the book. I hope you enjoy it!

-Aaron J. Lafazan, November 25th, 2015

CHAPTER 1

My Thoughts On Education

I 'm one of the crazy kids. I'm someone who trusts our youth today to succeed in an environment that they could potentially fail in.

In my mind, education should be a top priority of the United States, to ensure that our future generations are prepared enough to succeed and thrive in a tough and always-changing world. How can anyone expect kids to do well in life if they are being treated like toddlers, in that their learning is based off of flash cards instead of real-life learning?

Now, I actually think that middle school is more important than high school, and even college, for many reasons. First off, middle school is the first place that sets your developmental pattern for the rest of your life. You develop habits, mindsets, and attitudes you'll be stuck with for the rest of your life. As such, we need to provide middle school students with the best possible curriculum and resources in order to ensure positive development. I realized this when I first entered 9th grade, during first period on the first day in high school, where I managed to already fall behind the rest of my class in 40 minutes. I was so lost, and the whole class was as well, because the information in high school was so *hard*. It was something we've never seen before: **a challenge.** As such, we had to work twice as hard to produce the same result in math. That's when I knew middle school was *really* important.

My favorite line about education is this: *there are no flash cards in life!* Life is not set in stone; something is always changing, something is always not as you thought it was going to be, and in reality, the only way to prepare kids for the future is by giving them the building blocks they need to succeed, to which they can then *manipulate these skills on their own.* We need to provide students with the necessary 'tools' so that students themselves can put these 'blocks' together. After all, students can't memorize their life.

Now, it is my belief that students need real world teaching in a real world way.

Students can't succeed in life unless they have the necessary knowledge that they can then apply on their own. This includes everything from entrepreneurship skills to public speaking. By giving students the ability to utilize their knowledge in many different aspects of life, they'll have the best chance to succeed in today's world.

Likewise, students need to be taught appropriate 21st century skills, in a balanced manner. Paul Graham said it best: "I'm sure there are lots of things kids should be taught that they aren't. The combination of forces that produced the default curriculum was so random, and the people teaching it are often so bad. So if there's one thing I'd tell kids, it's that they shouldn't assume that the things they're being taught are the most important things they could be learning. Intellectually ambitious kids have to take charge of their own education. Which doesn't mean ignoring the things they're taught in school so much as supplementing them with what they're not getting.

In a way it's unfortunate that kids have to do this - that schools aren't good enough that kids can just assume they're getting a 'balanced diet.' On the other hand, this is what all intellectually ambitious adults have to do. Maybe there are advantages to having to start early, at least for those who realize they have to."

Additionally, students need to be taught in a real world manner. As I mentioned earlier: students can't be taught to memorize, as there are no flash cards in life. As such, students need to obtain hands-on, practical learning, where they can learn by doing and discover things for themselves. They need to collaborate and bounce ideas off of each other; they need to work together to solve problems; they need to be able to use logical thinking and applied skills for success in any subject really.

I see it all around me. Kids who come out of Middle School, unable to do the things that could potentially make the biggest difference in their lives. They'd rather copy and paste a poem or argument than construct an idea of their own. So many students are doing so poorly in their everyday lives, because they lack the necessary abilities to do otherwise. And it's honestly a shame.

That's why the day I realized the value of education, I gave up on the education system entirely. It was just a random day, a day I had shared the entirety of with my very intelligent family, and throughout the time spent with them, I was just so encapsulated in the knowledge and ideas that were transmitted between family members. It was as if they had notes written on their hands, they knew so much about what they were talking about. In such a nonchalant manner, knowledge about the economy and politics and social current events was shared. It covered everything really. I knew then 2 things for sure.

First, that I hadn't learned a thing in middle school, because even some parts of the conversation came up about things like logic and my brothers were arguing over a stupid math thing, and I didn't know *anything* about what they were saying.

The second thing I learned was that I wanted to be like that, *educated*. But, because of the lackluster ability of the US education system to properly educate me, I decided to educate myself, to learn *the right way*. The single best decision I've ever made. One day, I picked a move right out of John Locke's book, and decided to go explore the world, and learn for myself. I started businesses. I watched talks about the economy, and was able to talk with those around me about it. I wrote a book! I learned about financially literacy. I became an entrepreneur. I made myself a 21st century ready kid.

Now, I still go to school, but honestly, I am just so disappointed with the education system. I am unable to be fed the knowledge I am so eager to obtain. I love learning, I really do. I honestly try to learn something new every day. But, when I found that school couldn't give me what I sought, I set out on my own path to create who I am today.

That was actually the foundation for this book, to take what I've learned and done for myself, and apply it to our education system. Because I want to see a change in our school curriculum.

With this book, I want to have students take away that it's ok to learn something different than in school, to learn that what they know is probably very little, and to learn how to make a change.

Also, I want educators to take away that they do nothing to help young students in middle school *advance*, and that I have given up on you.

So, let's make a splash; let's change the way we educate, especially with the essential skills that comprise 90% of the rest of the book.

CHAPTER 2

Writing

Writing is a necessary and valuable skill required by all people in life who want to be successful. It is important for all walks of life, yet it certainly was not taught as it should have been in Middle School. This is because writing in secondary schools is much less productive than it should have been.

Writing Constraints In School

Let's first address the kind of writing we were tasked with, in 3 words: **Essay After Essay.** Whether it was a compare-and-contrast essay, relating to your own life, or even a historical DBQ (Document-Based Question) in social studies class, almost every piece of assigned writing revolved around *the essay*. Don't get me wrong; essays are extremely important. They're supposed to be an extensive discourse on a particular subject, which allows for an incredibly wide range of discussion. But they have a number of major downsides that most people fail to see.

Many students say that the biggest problem with essay writing is the format. Each year, a new strange format would be taught and was expected to be implemented, such as the 'RICH' and 'RAFT' styles. I would tell you what they stand for, but I honestly don't even remember myself! This is simply not how writing should be taught! Writing isn't about formats and guidelines; it is supposed to be your own voice, expressed how you deem it should be best presented. After all, the captain of the ship always controls the flow of the boat, so why can't students, the captains of their writing, control the flow?

If you write a beautiful piece, and feel that you should rearrange details based on importance or segue into paragraphs that help the writing flow best, than no one should stop you. In my opinion, along with many of my peers, writing is a way to express how you feel about a topic. Whether it is a persuasive essay to legalize a new medicine or to prove points when discussing the best course for military action in the Middle East, it is an opinion. No one can take that away from you. Except Middle School teachers.

These teachers reinforce different types of formats, grading you on what they believe to be best. Students should have been graded on content, rather than style, but were not. Instead, those who most closely adhered to the teacher's outline and essay criteria achieved high scores.

Each year, in our school, we received a new teacher, complete with a new set of ideas and instructions as to how they thought an essay should be constructed. This is frustrating for a student who is trying to build skills based on the previous years' learning. If often appears that each year *contradicts* all the prior year's schoolings. After students finally master one of the many types of writing introduced by any given teacher, they are then forced to do a complete 180 the following year! Teachers overall are just not concerned with this, and it ends up severely hurting the student.

When you teach a student how to complete a math problem, or how to take notes on a reading in Social Studies, you are teaching them a definitive way to achieve a specific goal, one they will likely remember for a long time. However, when you contradict what is taught every year, not only is it challenging, but quite frankly, it compromises the student's ability to perform well in class. Imagine being forced to learn a new way of doing the same thing, over and over. It is reverse motivation. After a while, one question comes to mind: 'What's the Point?' And if students are focused on this instead of the task at hand then I would suggest that there's a problem.

The second definition of essay is a very apt definition in this situation: "An Attempt Or Try." Essays define what teachers are *attempting* to have the whole class replicate given models so that everyone can receive an A+ on the upcoming State Test. In New York, State Tests for English are basically essay responses to an assigned reading. In a nutshell, students are asked a question given to them based on other readings they provide you, and students then have to use the author's words to comprise an essay. Teachers instruct students to generally formulate a conglomeration of what was presented in the assigned passage, paraphrased. It is a test of comprehension and not of writing skills. So, this aspect of teaching essays is another reason why this type of writing cannot be taught.

While on the subject of Essays, there's also the associated assigned vocabulary, which was only stressed because it was usually on or expected to be featured on the end result of the state test. In regards to utilizing the vocabulary, creativity is not relevant; there is no credit given for creative writing skills, and furthermore, creative writing is not expected. Students are just expected to memorize a few hundred vocab words and apply them in a way that is applicable even in the slightest sense.

I for one, blame the education system. Writing in middle schools has not changed much in the last 100 years and teachers themselves rarely deviate from the current agenda. A format exists for testing and the teaching curriculum is built around that. End of story. And as students, we are expected to conform. In matter of fact, one of the main problems with writing stems from the teachers, in regards to their teachings.

This can be a disadvantage as one enters high school. In regards to myself, I found the transition rather difficult. Rather than the monotonous, 'keyed' writing styles we were introduced to and taught, I now expected to churn out an original, voice-oriented piece. This can be a challenge at times for anyone, but it is even more arduous when one has little to no experience in creative writing.

Time constraints further complicate essay writing. Yes, many things in life do have time limits, and students need to learn to handle these deadlines, but too many problems arise when you are allotted only 40 minutes of class time to read documents and write an entire essay, or even compose a Document-Based-Question response. These types of writings are extremely hurtful for students; for instance, many students won't have a full understanding of what they are reading if they have such little time to comprehend the writing. What is the purpose of giving kids an assignment to complete without allowing the required time to comprehend what they are reading, never mind respond to questions? Shouldn't the goal of education be more than skimming text and the regurgitation of the words using quotation marks?

I think writing is supposed to be so much more; to me, it's the simple and elegant flow of words created when you string together a highly intellectual sentence. It's the voice expressed when you attempt to persuade your reader to side with your point of view.

The best writers have a charisma that jumps off the page, grabs you, and pulls you in. This is how we should learn to write. If we are not teaching kids to write this way, we are doing them a disservice. This is why we need to learn to write, to *really write.*

Alternative Narratives

There are many new types of writing, which should and could easily be implemented and acquired in Middle School; such included in this book are opinionated writing, storytelling, and creative writing.

Opinionated Writing

One type of alternative writing is Opinionated Writing. This type of writing would focus on events that are happening in today's society, or simply any open-ended question. Yes, important lessons are taught and derived from older texts, but unfortunately students don't feel like they apply in today's world. They don't see the relevancy. In fact, I don't think there is even any relevancy to writing and reading about older texts! I once asked a teacher why the next book we were going to read in class was an older, boring book instead of a fresh and hot one. She responded with, "Because you should know it for society." Should we really be prioritizing something in our schools simply for the sake of knowledge, with no application in sight?

What students need are the study of more modern texts and current events, which convey information that will contribute to the development of ideas and opinions. Once an opinion exists, then a student has a voice, and they can then grow his or her voice. Isn't that the goal of writing?

This type of Opinionated Writing allows students to express their thoughts, ideas, and beliefs. This freely written response is important for kids to learn how to express themselves in later life, which could also lead to a better rendering of a presentation in Speech and Debate, which is prevalent in too many walks of life to exist.

Speech and Debate is all about getting your ideas across to whoever is listening. By providing students with an outlet for them to put their thoughts to paper, it also provides both the ignition and the content that may be used for oral presentations. Many good speakers are great writers, and I know personally that if creative writing had been implemented in Middle School, I would have benefitted greatly in many areas of my life.

A big possibility in regards to opinionated writing could be having students writing pieces about their thoughts on certain current events. In my mind, at least, I feel that a current events portion of writing/English class would be greatly important, as it kills multiple birds with one stone.

First off, current events themselves are extremely important to know about. The ability to discuss what is going on around you, and to actually know what you are saying, is so important, which I'll elaborate on more soon. Something crazy involving knowing the world around you: I actually didn't learn about 9/11 until I was in 4th grade. No one had bothered to tell me about it, and when I found out, I was so heartbroken, and I knew that I wish I would've known. You should always know the world you live in.

When you walk into an average middle school, high school, or even college classroom, chances are no one knows what's going on. As an example, in 9th grade, my great social studies teacher had this thing, where on all of her pop quizzes on homework due that day, the extra credit would always be a current event, something going on in the world. And nine out of ten times, no one would have any idea of the answers, some of which that had literally been on the news for the entirety of the 48 hours leading up to that class. And it's so terrible that this is reality, where so many people don't know what's going on in the world. There was a great article about this, written by Courtney James on her website, https://worldaffairscharlotte.wordpress.com, in which she explains the importance of current affairs:

"According to the Pew Research Center for the People and the Press indicated that public knowledge of current affairs have changed very little despite dramatic changes in the media and information revolution (2007). On average, today's citizens are about as able to name their leaders, and are about as aware of major news events, as was the public nearly 20 years ago.

Here are some reasons why you should stay informed on current events and global issues impacting the world we live in today:

To be part of the global community
Globalization is a reality! There is no choice but to be part of the world rather than stand alone. It's more important now to "connect the dots in what's becoming a very small world."

To build informed opinions
Gaining knowledge in world affairs and current events allows you to decide where you fall on key issues impacting your city, region and country. It also provides you the ability to influence legislators in a meaningful and thoughtful way. "Never doubt that a small group of thoughtful, committed citizens can change the world; indeed, it's the only thing that ever does" – Margaret Mead

To spark engaging discussion

Enjoy healthy debates or discussions with friends, colleagues and community groups to increase their knowledge (and yours) about issues like poverty, hunger, war and conflict, foreign policy and the world economy. Growing awareness is often built on these types of conversations!

To enhance your employment opportunities

Competition from professionals in the global market place is growing. It's increasingly vital to set yourself apart from your peers by displaying a broad understanding of international affairs and current events.

To learn about cultures outside of your own

You're likely to find people from many different countries in your home, school or work places with the influx of immigrants into the United States. By keeping up-to-date with current events, you have the opportunity to change your views on cultural stereotypes (if any) and learn about what's happening and what matters to the international communities in your respective towns and cities.

To prepare for travel

Being informed about a country before a visit can decrease unexpected "surprises" and travel mishaps (i.e. basic safety procedures.) In addition, keeping up with the news also allows you to get to know the country, people and cultures that you will encounter during your travels abroad.

'When you travel, you are humble and have empathy for other people...these are important life skills. When you travel, you can look at your own country from a distance and see the challenges at a higher contrast, and that helps you go home and help others who are dealing with the same problems.' – Rick Steves (quoted in Charlotte Weekly)."

I feel that this article by James was incredible in demonstrating the wide-ranging effects of being aware of current events.

Additionally, current events are an incredible target for opinionated writing, in that they spark the best prompts for student pieces.

I partake in the Forensics Speech & Debate club at my high school, which I've been doing about a year and a half so far. In this club, I mainly participate in an event entitled Extemporaneous Speaking. Here, students are tasked with 'drawing' a question about any possible current event at that time, and formulating a seven-minute oral speech on it in 30 minutes. Thus, when doing your best to work under the event's parameters, my competitors and I alike are forced to know about what's going about almost everything going on in the world, even if it's just an idea of what's happening or knowing everything in regards to that topic. I find this event to be so great, not only because of the fact that knowing current events I am able to do / be prepared for everything in the aforementioned article, but additionally, I find myself given real, thought-provoking, and almost exciting questions. It's a crazy concept, yes, but I love the event, because it allows me the opportunity to think for myself and construct a well-developed argument about anything, and then share my opinions with those around me. These types of encounters are what I seek to have more often, especially for middle school writing. In middle school, and in most writings, most prompts are extremely boring, and make me hate to write. Such include, 'List a common theme between the two (boring) pieces of work and develop it with strong information,' or, 'What is one way in which Sally was able to conquer her dreams? Did she go about doing it in the right way?' and stuff like that. These types of questions boil my blood; if you're going to make kids write for forty minutes straight, and possibly risk having students get carpel tunnel, why not give a good essay prompt? And that's exactly what current events do. They provide an incredible opportunity for thought-provoking, individualized responses for questions like, "Would you put boots on the ground to fight ISIS?" or, "Would you raise the minimum wage?" These types of questions provide for a chance to develop a well-thought out answer with real points, and an easy format for which to answer the question.

Here, I originally envisioned the teacher spending small amounts of time in class discussing specific current events, and then assigning thought-provoking questions based off of that topic, which would give kids an excuse to study current events and practice proper writing. But, even giving students articles to go along with the writing would be fine, as long as students have the ability to write something meaningful and something that actually relates to them.

Overall, I am all for teaching about current events, and feel the best way to accomplish this integration would be through English class with Opinionated Writing. After all, US Secretary of State Colin Powell once said that, "America's success abroad is founded on the rock of an informed and involved public," so why shouldn't we have kids partaking in current-event based knowledge?

Also, on that note of interesting prompts, the part of opinionated writing that I feel is most important is actually the prompt students are being asked to write about. I know from my experience, my essays' liveliness and overall greatness was 100% based off of the question at hand. If the prompt was exciting (it almost never was), than I would be excited to write, and I would really spend time reviewing my writing and ensuring that my arguments were 'on point'. However, when I receive a terrible prompt, as is the case 99% of the time, I was just uninterested to perform, to actually think about the question at hand and give a clear, thoughtful opinion piece.

That is why a large basis of opinionated writing needs to revolve around certain prompts. If teachers are going to create their own prompts, than they need to understand the importance of ensuring that students will be 'entertained' by the opinionated question at hand.

I came across this great article on this website, small-worldathome.blogspot.com, where this woman named Sarah provided 100 questions that could be used as interesting writing prompts. Some of them even made me stop and think what I would respond for a few of them. They included everything from asking students to write about past experiences to asking about students' thoughts about society's actions. Just to name a few, they include:

1.   Write about your first name—why you were given it, what associations or stories are attached to it, what you think or know it means. Do the same for your last name. What name would you give yourself other than the one you actually have?

2. Maya Angelou said "I've learned that you can tell a lot about a person by the way s/he handles these three things: a rainy day, lost luggage, and tangled Christmas tree lights." Tell a story in which a character has to deal with one, two, or all three of these scenarios. How does your character respond?

3. Write about someone who has no enemies. Is it even possible?

Just because you might be thinking of it now, yes, these aren't the most traditional representatives of 'opinion writing', but they do provide the opportunity for incredible creative writing of students in a somewhat opinionated matter. After all, the students are middle school kids; don't they deserve a little bit of unorthodox in their schooling.

As we can see with this incredible post, it really doesn't take much at the end of the day to create a captivating writing question, so why can't we do more of it?

Storytelling

Another type of writing that can be taught is Storytelling. Here, students would have to explain a series of events specific to a certain situation. This type of writing is used far more widely and frequently in everyday life than the kind of writing skills required to answer essay questions. An older friend of mine likes to say, "Some of the best writers and public speakers like to relate everything to telling a story." That's why stories flow so well; it's simply the elaboration of event after event. Each story illustrates what they're trying to express and the narrative is maintained through the telling and re-telling of different events.

This type of writing would promote and spark creativity among students, by encouraging them to use their own experiences to illustrate various points. It's the ability to roll with any concept, in any type of genre. This leads to innovative thinking. There's no better definition of creativity than putting a twist on a pre-existing occurrence. And this would be accomplished here, where the thought process in which new ideas are formulated, resulting in positive ideas overall.

Creative Writing

Yet another great idea for how to make the writing better for middle school students is 'Creative Writing'; now, the word 'creative' was thrown around a lot in the Opinionated Writing section, but this section is it's own part, so keep reading. According to one student, "Many kids dream of being writers and poets one day. I know I do. And because of this, more time should be spent on creative writing class. It also better prepares you for more advanced writing." Creative writing, simply put, makes you a better writer.

That's why the current system of writing isn't nearly as helpful as it could be, as most essays are written with the lack of implementation of differentiation. Imagine if you were in the shoes of the respective student here. You wish to become a Poet, or it is your life's dream to be a professional writer, yet your ability and passion aren't encouraged. This is because it goes against the current State Testing. You are told repeatedly to stick to a particular format, and only this format. If you stray, *you are penalized for creativity.* So when you choose to write on your own time, your heart tells you to write what it's feeling, but your subconscious tells you it's wrong. Your dream slips farther from your grasp and your greatest gift - creativity - begins to dwindle.

Is this really the result we are after? I think not. So, what do we need to do? Write creatively, write creatively, and then, write creatively; in order to implement this creativity in all aspects of life, we need to encourage this creativity in writing. Whether it is in English class or solving a curveball-problem in math to translating a sentence in a foreign language, the spark of new ideas can easily benefit everyone at hand. And best of all, it can be encouraged through a new style of writing taught in middle school.

Expert Opinions

Robert Marzano

Robert Marzano also had something to say about the subject of writing. Marzano is a premier educational expert in the United States, published in over thirty books and one hundred and fifty publications.

Marzano's opinion on writing is entirely different. He says that the focus of the subject should not be on writing for the sake of literature, as most people will not end up becoming novelists in the near future or even in the distant one! Instead, the focus in general should be on Expository writing. He explains that this ability to write a coherent claim, to make a statement and be able to back it up with hard evidence in an overall suitably written piece. This is important because this type of writing gets the brain flowing, and helps in the process of thinking and creation. Also, and perhaps more importantly, this is the type of writing most commonly found across most disciplines.

If you ask a teenager about their biggest problem with school, 90% of them will say, "I am never going to use what I am learning – it's a waste". But, if expository writing were implemented more than in the current curriculum, then we would see that students could be proven quite wrong. The ability to make a logical and coherent statement in a written piece on any topic and provide information backing up that claim is essential in almost every walk of life. If you become a scientist, and you make an incredible discovery, odds are you are going to need to write a convincing argument pertaining to your discovery. This will ensure your place in the history books! This is just one example, but this type of writing has many different applications in other professions, such as with Lawyers, Doctors, and Psychologists.

He also reiterated that emphasis should not be placed on story writing, simply because many will not dabble in this field in particular. However, Exposition is a widely prevalent and needed form of writing.

In addition, he says, exposition pieces are important because when writing them, or, for that matter, in regards to any form of writing, a key component to your work is overall logic. Through the use of logic, one is able to obtain information about the piece, and with this knowledge, the writer can construct the piece in a manner appropriate to their respective needs. For example, one instance that requires logic is knowing who the target audience is, and as such, a level of formality required for that specific audience needs to be achieved.

This can be demonstrated through the difference between texting and 'cold-emailing' (rather than 'cold-calling'). When texting, there is a different style of grammar utilized, another syntax of language entirely, and spelling is not a concern. However, when 'cold-emailing', a task that you might do in hopes of getting a company to interview you for a job, you have to ascertain what is necessary in order to write a powerful and effective email that will accomplish what you set out to do.

Now, obviously this is a minor example, but there are many other nuances that go into writing that simply need to be looked at and cared for through the utilization of logic. Overall, logic is used in writing as a blanket-like key ideology, utilized in order to understand and ascertain where certain rules apply in that work of literature.

Deborah Meier

When asked her thoughts about changing the writing system in primary schools, Deborah Meier immediately jumped on one specific topic: State tests. She made clear to me that state tests should be completely abolished. This is also something that I've championed since the formation of state mandated tests. In case you're lucky enough to not be subjected to state tests, let me explain. State tests are examinations mandated from the state in order to assess the performance of a teacher in a specific subject. Lately, state tests have been getting a little out of hand, at least in my opinion. In New York State, they are given in every subject, including Gym, where a test at the beginning of the year is given to set the baseline, and one is given at the end of the year to show improvement.

In addition to this, there is a huge problem with all of the extra testing that needs to be performed in middle school. In 8th grade alone, I took at least four different state examinations in English throughout the course of the year. Reading comprehension, essay writing, combinations of different genres. Everything was covered, but it didn't matter. According to Mrs. Meier, and most who seek state test reform, the tests are a poor way of assessing what the skills are of each individual student; as such, there is no point to the state tests. This is because what students are taught is based directly from what will be covered on the state test, and the teacher does not deviate from that topic.

State test are very restricting, says Meier, in that they do not help students take this time of their life to explore different styles of writing, and find which one best suits their individual voice. She suggested a simple yet popular solution to the problem of poor writing curriculum: Storytelling. Different ways of retelling stories, she says, is a skill that can be practiced to develop the best writer in all of us. Every age should incorporate storytelling in the curriculum, so that students who have the impulse and inclination to tell stories have their enthusiasm and passion for this is kept alive. Recounting a specific series of events, whether it is an accurate narrative or a simple imaginative story, is an art that deserves to be fostered.

This is especially important because of the fact that some people are natural storytellers. This concept of writing and expanding on a series of events has been with us since the beginning of time. It is how one generation passes information to the next; it is global; it transcends barriers of race, economics and religion. It is the most basic and the oldest form of communication. Storytelling is in our blood; it's what we are! So it is most certainly a necessity to have students practice, sample, and experiment with this expression of writing. Sharing our stories and our narratives connects us to each other and to the past, according to Meier.

Bill Ayers

Additionally, Bill Ayers believed that it is absolutely critical that all human beings learn to write and express themselves as early as possible. Ayers is a Distinguished Professor of Education and retired Senior University Scholar at the University of Illinois.

Ayers has three grandchildren, aged 11, 8, and 3 years old, and he states that at the core, all of them are writers and storytellers. Obviously, the 3 year old has more simple stories, while the 11 year old writes graphic novels pertaining to Middle School Life.

Ayers believes proper instruction in writing is critical because it is a fundamental form of human expression. In the process of expressing ideas, it creates the intellectual fuel that keeps the mind sharp. He believes that Middle Schools needs to allow young people to tell stories, find their voices, and express themselves in a variety of forms. He also talks about the fact that young people should write in order to reflect on subjects, on history, and to be competent in their ability to share their opinions.

Ayers began to share insight in regards to writing as a whole. He talked about how preschoolers, young kids who have no worries on their minds, are not constantly criticized about syntax and punctuation, but are simply encouraged to convey their thoughts in any way they can. Over time, as these young children blossom into young adulthood, they find ways to correct themselves, to catch their mistakes, and overall perfect their craft to the best of their ability.

Mr. Ayers believes this is a type of practice that more and more middle schools should incorporate. Students should not necessarily focus 100% of their efforts solely on the grammatical part of writing. Instead, students should concentrate on presenting ideas, on being able to express themselves and tell a better story more effectively. After all, the best stories aren't the ones that are the most grammatically correct; they are the ones whose plots are the most interesting, whose stories are most fun to retell, the literature that excites the reader. The form of communication to focus on should be more about presenting ideas in a positive manner, as opposed to worry about being syntactically right. After all, writing is neither technical nor linear. Writing, says Ayers, is about thinking in its deepest form, about exploration into a field that may be different than originally thought, about taking a seed and watching it grow and blossom in to a beautiful flower.

To illustrate his point of what he believes should be focused on in writing, Ayers began to give personal examples of his findings. He shared how a member of his family began to write a story about a blind 16 year old. She soon realized that the best writers are those that experience what their characters are experiencing firsthand, and so she decided to try to experience what it is like to be blind. This opened her eyes, so to speak, to the world around her, and forced her to operate and live in a completely different way. She began to see the world around her in a completely different light. No pun intended.

Another personal example in Ayer's findings came from when he worked at a detention center in Chicago for troubled youth. Although he had taught every level of school, he soon discovered this experience would be like no other. Many of the kids at this detention center were, for the most part, illiterate. However, Ayers discovered that if he could prompt and encourage these kids to talk about and to share their feelings, they could soon tell their stories in an incredible way. He found that these kids could communicate to the outside world, specifically to their parents and their siblings. All he would do was ask the kids a question or two, or even have the kids dictate what they wanted to share, and he found that these kids could recite words that Ayers would then capture with grace and fluidity.

These troubled youths could elaborate and share opinions, not through the written word, but through spoken word, which was then converted to the written word. It could then be shared with the intended recipients. This type of assistance became truly important to them, as here, storytelling became the vehicle for them to learn how to read and write. It provided incentive and it gave them something to look forward to, as well as creating an opportunity that had not existed previously: they were able share their stories with others.

This is why writing is so important. It's because everyone has a story to tell, or an experience to share, and writing that is the medium through which these pieces travel.

Conclusion

Enid Bagnold, a British author and playwright, once said, "Who wants to become a writer? And why? Because it's the answer to everything… It's the streaming reason for living. To note, to pin down, to build up, to create, to be astonished at nothing, to cherish the oddities, to let nothing go down the drain, to make something, to make a great flower out of life, even it it's a cactus."

Effective and Incredible writing is one of the most important 21st century skills kids need to have, and as such, writing in Middle Schools needs to be changed.

CHAPTER 3

Foreign Language

4 0 minutes a day, 180 days a year, for 3 years. That's 21,600 minutes, 360 hours, or 15 days, whichever way you wish to look at it. That's the total amount of time middle school students were forced to sit through their foreign language class and do nothing. Fifteen entire days of Spanish class, and nothing positive came out of it!

Imagine what you could do in fifteen days. In three days, groups of teenagers in events called 'hackathons' can come up with plans for nuclear reactors, statistical investing platforms, programs that change the way you operate mechanical systems at home, and so much more. Imagine the capabilities for kids when given five times that amount!

Learning a Foreign Language

A lo largo de mi experiencia de la escuela intermedia, una cosa que he aprendido a gusto y aprecio es lengua.

Spanish translation: Throughout my middle school experience, I've come to appreciate being multi-lingual. In my school specifically, we were given the option to pick one language, either Spanish, Italian, or French, and follow it through the next 7 years of our learning career. We started early in 6th grade, at the beginning of middle school, and will continue through our senior year in high school, However, I believe the way we were taught foreign language was inefficient.

Language Study in Middle School

Most will agree that one goal or benefit of learning a foreign language is having the ability to go abroad and converse with locals. Of course, this doesn't necessarily imply speaking like a native of that region. I mean, no one expects any student to be as fluent as a local; but, it does imply that you should have a more comprehensive understanding than knowing how to say 'Where's the bathroom?' and 'What is your name?'

The goal when learning a second or third language is to be fluent. Wherever you travel, you should be able to immerse yourself in exciting new places, meet new people, and have tons of fun! But I feel that this opportunity was denied to kids in Middle School; if the goal was for us to achieve some level of conversational Spanish, it was simply not met. This is why the middle school language classes can be defined by most, including myself, as 'Shockingly Useless' and 'Writing-based' to most kids.

In each language, students were taught the same simple concepts. We learned very specific nouns you would rarely use, such as the name of every animal on the planet, verbs like 'to scuba dive' and simple phrases like 'where's the desk?' There were entire stretches of time, spanning several weeks, where we would work on one simple, seemingly irrelevant subject, such as watersports, or like when we studied emotions for a month and a half, and learned how to introduce yourself to someone and ask their name in return *in the same amount of time*. We spent hours learning these parts of the language when it could have been accomplished in much less time.

If you broke down what we did learn in our middle school career, it's the most inefficient curriculum in existence. At the end of the day, we had acquired an incredibly large and seemingly useless vocabulary. Which brings us back to my initial point: the struggle to achieve conversational speech. When we did attempt to converse with our classmates, we were god-awful. With our tongues moving at a snail's pace of about 3 words a minute, and the added pressure of the teacher being within earshot (who may be taking points off your participation grade if she didn't like what she heard) most of us were reduced to babbling idiots.

Compare that to when you were just beginning school and barely spoke English. Imagine your Preschool teacher attempting to teach you English for the first time, but instead of encouraging you to speak, your teacher just gave you worksheets to learn English. Yes, you might have an incredible vocabulary, but you would also be incapable of expressing your thoughts. Having a vocabulary is useless unless one can use it appropriately in a conversation. Fast-forward to the present for my classmates and I; we are simply incapable of dialogue, since we weren't given the right tools to succeed! We need to teach kids a second language just as we were taught our first: by speaking it!

In the middle of 9th grade, a full three and a half years of "studying" Spanish under my belt, my family took a vacation in Mexico during Christmas break. Yes, the trip was great; I had a fun time, everyone was happy. You know what could've made the trip even better than it already was? If I had been able to speak Spanish!!

At the time I was one of the most fluent speakers in my grade, even winning the Spanish Award at the end of the year. Yet, when I arrived in Mexico, I was dumbfounded. The entirety of what I learned fell by the wayside. People all around me were speaking at lightning speed – and then there was me. In that moment, I realized I had not been taught conversational Spanish in a way that was practical. Forget vocabulary, forget verb tenses; the local population did not even adhere to the rules I was taught in middle school!

I was given precious workbooks to learn "the true side of the language," most of which had information that had never even been heard of by the locals. I showed one waiter some of my Spanish homework, and he gave me the weirdest look. I might as well have asked him, "Can you direct me to Mars?" and his reaction would have been the same. This experience was hugely disappointing, as it showed me that despite wanting to learn a language, and putting in the time, I had not. Every kid coming out of 8th grade should have the ability to converse in a foreign language. It's more than my opinion; it's my demand!

It is critical that when language is taught as a second language the approach should focus on teaching conversational Spanish, etc. Currently we are writing mediocre essays, when we could be learning to converse on everyday topics.

One thing that should be immediately focused on is the teaching itself: *what* and *how* students are taught a foreign language.

Now, let's talk about the *what*. We need a greater focus to be placed on speaking the language, not memorizing vocab. Here I reiterate; the way we are taught now is not educating us properly. We cannot continue the ways of the past, as they are not serving us in the present. It's time to focus creating something better for the future.

My Dream for Learning Language Fluently

Over the course of writing this book, I came up with an idea, a program of sorts, one that I would really like to see implemented. I call it, "The Lafazan Basic Fluency Program," and it comprises of a number of different basic concepts.

Firstly, I only want our foreign language teachers implementing at most 5 units throughout our entire middle school career. And none of it should be complicated – just the conversational basics. Familiarities and simple communication vocabulary should be the main focus. Then we get into practicing dialogue, dialogue, and more dialogue.

Once the students develop a solid foundation in conversing, and they have proven that they understand language concepts, then we can see the emergence of truly multi-lingual students. And after the fluency is established, we can implement more complex vocabulary, and increase the level of complexity of the overall nature of the class over time. Why are we throwing hard and impractical vocabulary at kids first, rather than providing simple access to the language?

Now, let's focus on the *how*. One way to change how we teach language is by changing the way our teachers test the student's knowledge of the language-at-hand. The main focus of grades should be derived specifically from the following, in order to ensure that students are being tested properly, and thus have the best chance to learn from mistakes and get real feedback:

1)   The Dialogue of the Conversation

2)   The Fluency the Dialogue Provides

Dialogue of the Conversation

For the rest of this section, I am going to refer to Dialogue as the actual words the student is speaking.

Now, I feel the dialogue of the foreign language conversation is incredibly important, in order to ensure our students are making sense. We need to ensure that middle school students can translate the type of conversation they would use in every day English. They should be able to convey their points and messages clearly and concisely.

Fluency of Dialogue

We want to ensure that our students can convey a message clearly and concisely. When you're talking with a friend, or really talking about anything in general, it's not a good idea to mumble. It's important that people understand what you're saying. I wish I had known that I was not expected to speak as quickly as the people I hear on TV or those to whom Spanish is their native tongue. After all, speaking slowly is part of the learning process and promotes clarity.

In addition, I was also intimidated when the teacher listened to our verbal exercises. Teachers should of course be able to observe and participate in dialogue; however, teachers should in no way place grades or any pressure at all among students during their conversations. With this, fluency of the dialogue needs to be carefully instructed and practiced.

Implementation of the Lafazan Basic Fluency Program

To implement "The Program" we must address how the teachers should monitor students. I am going to assume that all teachers following this plan are totally committed to their students, because that is the only way the program works.

Firstly, under this program, teachers need to implement what I call "The Milestone Test". Basically, it would be an end-of-the-week assessment, which would be done at random, and would assess the student's conversational abilities: to speak and be understood, and to listen and understand.

By approaching it in this manner, it promotes a more natural style of conversation rather than a scripted one based on notes. Providing assessed feedback rather than a grade also alleviates a lot of the pressure associated with foreign language in school, so kids feel less nervous and are more likely to speak more freely. It could last a minute for each student, whether it be face to face in class, while other kids are practicing, or through technology, like with Google Voice.

I'm sure that if this program is implemented, teachers will get a crystal clear image of where their students are in their learning process. From there, you can assess the needs and gaps in their knowledge. This will allow for personalized tips on how to speak and what to say and address common mistakes. That's the key to deeper learning.

An even better way to implement the deepest learning possible for students is to have the class conducted entirely, or mostly, in Spanish early on. It's important for kids to be totally immersed in what they are doing, which will give them the best kind of environment to successfully learn the foreign language. As of now, the middle school classes are mainly taught in English. Some teachers try to use more Spanish than others, but it is inconsistent which is not conducive to actively learning the language.

Middle School Classes Today

A normal middle school foreign language class revolves around a Question & Answer format between students and teachers. Everything is conducted in English, with the exception being the answer to the question at hand. You'd be surprised how little that foreign language is actually spoken. If we are only speaking in English, then what are we learning? Nothing. That's why I recommend the class be taught almost entirely in Spanish. Immersing the students in the language is the best opportunity for success. I do suggest that *some* English be used initially, but then phased out gradually as one moves up in grade, so that the end of middle school teaches the class entirely in Spanish. That's how you win it – yes, some kids will get lost, some kids will get confused, but it provides the best pathway for learning the language all in all.

Along with the lack of conversation comes the problem of 'vocab sheets'; an overwhelming amount of these annoyingly lengthy papers are given to students. In fact, memorizing the vocab sheet in middle school would probably have led to more class success than knowing how to use it in that foreign language. To combat this problem, I would stop the distribution of vocab sheets and get rid of them entirely. What we need is to practice dialogue, practice dialogue, and then practice dialogue a little more. Useless vocabulary is, well, useless. An extensive vocabulary does not make one a great conversationalist. As a student, I can say we were more concerned with memorizing the vocab sheet at hand than anything else, for the sake of our grades. We worried about memorizing the definition of each word rather than how to apply it in conversation.

Additionally, teachers also have to start showing student's videos and clips and activities in the foreign language they're learning. A big problem I still face is that most kids learning a 2nd language are always trying to translate the conversation from that language to English and do the reverse when trying to speak. I personally figure out what I'm going to say in English, translate it to Spanish, spit it out, and repeat. Pretty inefficient. However, if middle school classes were to watch the news, among many other types of immersive programs, in a foreign language, you could begin to develop an ear for it and start to think in a more creative and direct way. As an example, for a lesson about transportation, students should be shown clips about happenings in transportation in foreign countries, in that foreign language. TV and news could be shown to students in class, and Spanish music could be played. Only by doing this can students start to think in a different language, which makes it so much easier for communication.

Finally, a part of my vision is much in-class dialogue with "Partner Prompts". This is my solution to speaking often and fluently. In class, real-life situations and scenarios would be distributed, with students being given a prompt and asked to carry out a conversation with their partner. I'm not saying it has to be graded; I'd rather it wasn't, but I am saying students need to practice. Language is a skill, and it requires time and repetition. It may be scary for students to speak to teachers; it may be difficult to envision a real-life scenario when speaking on the phone. However, when speaking to a classmate, one can learn to converse with ease. As an example partner prompt:

Situation:
Person A: You are a tourist visiting Portugal, and you're lost. You can't find your way to meet your way to meet your family, who are waiting for you. The address is 123 Doodleberry Lane. You also have not planned an itinerary for the trip, and your wife is going to get very upset when she finds out.

<u>Person B</u>: You are a native of the land, who is familiar with the address and provides directions. In turn, you must also ask the man questions pertaining to his trip, and answer his questions about the city and activities to do.

Simple activities like this one I just illustrated could be very beneficial to students, and can play a very large role in a student's ability to learn a foreign language.

To summarize, students need to be given end-of-the-week-assessments, the teaching environment needs to change, and we need to incorporate daily student-to-student interaction. This is, I believe, the key to foreign language success, and this format should be strictly adhered to. If it was, I believe that graduates of middle school would be exponentially more multi-lingual, and not just by getting by, but by being fluent. *Overall, Implementation of this program would be a game changer.*

Moving Forward with the Lafazan Basic Fluency Program

It is surprising that this these programs are not the current focus. These key elements in molding students of language are incredibly important. Teachers need to start assessing their lessons in foreign language; otherwise, the student in question will turn out mediocre-at-best (like 99% turn out now).

One thing many people don't realize is that it's much easier to speak fluently and to supplement that speaking with content, once fluency is attained, rather than being bombarded first with vocab and then expected to become fluent. It is much easier to implement the body of the text if you can speak fluently, rather than having to learn vocabulary day-after-day and not being able to speak a lick of the language. If teachers and students could teach and be taught in the plan just laid out, more people would be multi-lingual.

When learning English as a young kid, you were brought up with your surroundings in English, encapsulated with every aspect of that language everywhere you went. Only after being fully immersed were you able to comprehend it. That is what we need to do with foreign language! We need to get our students feeling like natives, or as close to it as we can possibly get, so that the second language becomes second nature. They need to eat it, sleep it, think it and dream in it. If we can properly immerse them, and implement a program designed to simulate the way we learned English as children, we would be able capitalize on our students' abilities to learn another language.

Learning a foreign language is actually very easy, when you understand that conversational language is important. This can be achieved when you physically travel to a foreign land, and are surrounded by people speaking the local language. This experience can be duplicated to some extent in the classroom, but must first be accepted as the preferred method of instruction. To learn it, you simply have to surround yourself with it.

Upon the completion of a middle school language class, one should have the ability to immerse themselves with confidence in the realm of discussion and *thrive*. As one student commented, 'I should leave Spanish Class and be able to go to Spain and blend in and be a native; I don't feel this way now though!' We need to change the way foreign language is taught in middle school to ensure their academic success in this field of study.

Expert Opinions

Deborah Meier

According to Meier, when asked what young kids should study, as well as how they should be taught regarding Foreign Language, very insightful points were made.

To begin with, she said, it is common knowledge that language, or almost everything, for that matter, is best learned through immersion, very much as with the *sink or swim* analogy. Many things are best learned with a hands-on approach, when fully immersed in the climate and the culture at hand. However, the dilemma that arises when faced with total immersion is that it is extremely difficult to artificially manufacture these settings. For example, if you wanted to learn Mandarin, obviously your best bet would be to take a trip to China, and immerse yourself in the language and the culture.

However, trying to recreate the surroundings you would encounter in a foreign country in a 15' by 15' classroom is next to impossible. This is why, Meier points out, we need to utilize our own communities, and the opportunities that do exist. Obviously, not every community can provide this type of experience for a student, but where possible, it would most certainly make a noticeable difference.

In addition to this possible solution of community-involvement, it was also pointed out how we need to find ways to bring people together to speak languages, which would assist in simulating cultural immersion. According to Meier, this would accomplish two main things:

> 1) It would help spur the process of learning of that specific foreign language, and help master it with regards to fluency and authenticity.

> 2) It would provide a wonderful opportunity to immerse young people into different cultures and different languages

After discussing some of the more general abstractions pertaining to changing the way foreign languages are taught, Ms. Meier went on to discuss foreign language on a personal level. Initially, she discussed how her grandchildren spent a year living in Ecuador. She said living in a foreign country and being surrounded by all of the ideologies and teachings that resulted from this was so beneficial to them. I completely concur with this, in that those who are fortunate enough to partake in this kind of adventures are given a marvelous gift of a great setting to practice foreign language. They are almost guaranteed to learn that language in the most realistic and proper way possible.

Additionally, Meier went into detail about her own life experiences. After studying Spanish for five years, she was placed in a Spanish speaking community in Harlem, where she was teaching. Meier said that when she first arrived, she was completely lost. Even though she had been learning Spanish for quite some time, nothing prepared her for the reality of speaking with others on a daily basis about day-to-day activities. Mrs. Meier was working in East Harlem in New York, at a time where Spanish was spoken by an incredible amount of the population. In order to communicate with the community, Ms. Meier needed to learn to speak Spanish.

To accomplish this goal, Meier took a trip for two months to Guatemala, to help with her foreign language skills. In her experience, this was a marvelous way to learn a language. Meier had lived with a family, obtained a tutor to facilitate her linguistic transition, and proceeded to explore the country with her tutor. Meier had studied the language through sightseeing, eating lunch at different restaurants in different parts of the country, visiting attractions as far away as the outskirts of the region, and most of all, talking to locals and discussing local events and local surroundings. They spoke in Spanish about what they were doing, and what their current or next exploration entailed.

She said this benefitted her greatly. She was able to practice the fluency of the language itself, and she also had real-life scenarios to discuss in Spanish. She pointed out that by talking about real things, you begin to understand more of what you are talking about, because it is literally exactly what you're doing. Partaking in those activities and elaborating on them in a foreign language allowed for her to subconsciously learn Spanish, and she began to understand her surroundings and become more fluent in both speech and thought with Spanish.

From firsthand experience, Meier was able to elaborate on the fact that you can imitate a language and all of the nuances associated with learning that language in an authentic way, by plunging in head first and trying new and exciting things. She points out that kids need to stop worrying about being thought of as stupid, and focus on what's important: trying to understand the language, and learning it through authenticity.

Meier's observations support my theory that complete immersion is the way to go, or as close to it as one can get. This would entail utilizing explorations that are usually possible in the real world and simulating them in an open and free classroom environment, instead of utilizing a textbook's resource of filling in blanks of a paragraph, as an example. By marinating in the language and the culture, one has greater chance of absorbing the language its nuances.

There are some challenges with this method learning, just as with any other, that Meier brought up.

For example, all languages have dialects. Spanish alone has about 10 different dialects, according to an article on http://www.altalang.com. Each different dialect is very different depending on where it is spoken, and this presents a problem: Which dialect do students learn? My answer: whichever one is spoken by the most people worldwide.

In addition, foreign languages are often different in other ways. Speed, cadence, and rhythm vary from country to another even when the language is the same. However, generally speaking, each language has one main form, and everything else that follows is a derivative. There is often an "official" format that is spoken and understood by most and then additional dialects that are understood regionally. If the "official" language is taught, then one has a significant change of being understood by a significant portion of the population.

Bill Ayers

Ayers believes that the learning of other languages is of critical importance to students. This is because the learning of foreign languages can positively influence the formation of the mind, increase your capacity to think, and allows you to think laterally, or in more creative ways than you would as a unilingual speaker.

Ayer's believes that foreign language is a matter of stepping into another culture, of being able to view the world through the eyes of another culture. He thinks that one of the fun aspects of learning a foreign language, in his opinion, is the realization of the many ways of seeing the world, which helps to overcome narcissism in life. We gain insight and new perspectives that would otherwise be impossible.

Ayers illustrated this point with a story of when he was travelling Egypt with a friend, who happened to be an Atheist. While in Egypt, Ayers would listen to his friend speak to the locals to obtain travel advice, directions, and other recommendations. He soon noticed his friend and whomever she was speaking with frequently used the phrases 'God willing' or 'God Blessing', as well as other similar phrases that referenced God. 'God willing, you can get to the restaurant by driving 10 miles.' 'God blessing, you could stay at that hotel for a cheap price.' He noticed these references, and knowing she was an Atheist, he found it to be quite odd. When asked about why she mentioned God so many times in her conversations, she answered that it was simply part of the culture to reference the higher being – it was the framing of the language to mention God in an incredibly prevalent way.

This is just one example how learning another language teaches one about another culture in a way that cannot simply be taught. You begin to walk in the shoes of another culture entirely, and begin to understand the nuances and complexities. In totality, the larger point Ayers made by telling the story was the association of learning these foreign languages with the act of recognition, with an act of respect. This allows us to move beyond our natural narcissism in order to succeed in new areas and in new ways, shedding light on new ideas. This is why learning a foreign language and learning about different cultures is so important, and can produce positive results in all aspects of life and also contribute to the success of young students.

Ayers also said that he wished people, including himself, didn't judge people of various nationalities so harshly as youths. He believes that learning other languages provides insight into other cultures that would alleviate some of the biases that exist today. It opens one's eyes in a way that cannot be recreated in a classroom. This would then allow people to integrate with other cultures and aspects of society more fully. This in turn would make for greater understanding on an international scale.

Additionally, according to Ayers, middle school curriculum should incorporate a wider range of language classes and opportunities. At my middle school, I was fortunate enough to have the possibility to choose to focus on any one of the following: Spanish, Italian, or French. However, Ayers believes that even this is not broad enough for middle schools. Ayers believes that curriculums should also include, Mandarin Chinese, Japanese, and American Sign Language, among others.

Language brings with it the nuances of the culture it defines. When we learn a new language, we experience and absorb all that culture has to offer; what is revered, what is respected, and what is paramount.

Conclusion

Foreign Language is an extremely valuable 21st century skill, one that needs to be focused on more in middle schools to adapt toward *conversational learning.*

CHAPTER 4

Communication Skills

Another important skill that all kids should have coming out of Middle school is to be proficient in all aspects of Communication, both verbal and nonverbal.

Communication is at the core of human behavior. Although it exists in many forms, it's the glue that binds our society together, be it through conversation, a power point presentation, an editorial essay, or a public speech at the local community center. Communication is central to society and needs to be taught in middle schools today.

Communication is more than just an exchange of information. It is about understanding the emotion as well as the intent behind the information at hand; after all, 90% of miscommunication is a result of misinterpretation. This emphasizes the need for which effective communication should be taught in middle schools. Effective communication allows the conveyance of a message so that in all of its totality, the message is received and understood, in the way it was intended.

My Experience In Developing Communication Skills

As we all know, the ability to communicate well is not as easy as it sounds. I can tell you of the countless number of times where I would be texting a friend or family member and there was a complete misunderstanding, or where I would be giving a presentation where I did not convey my own ideas properly. I have written emails that made so much sense to me and yet were complete and utter nonsense to anyone else. Even when I began to write this book, so many thoughts and ideas that I believed I had interpreted perfectly fell flat when I put pen to page (or fingers to keyboard, as the case may be). I am sure this has happened to you at some point or another; after all, it is a part of our life. Each and every day we all contribute to multiple miscommunications. Some are trivial and others are not; we just need to teach middle school students how to best avoid these problems, in order to alleviate the problem as best as we can, with the help of a communication class or segment.

Now, I know that to some, this chapter may not seem like a big deal. Honestly, who cares about communication? Well, I do. And I think you'll find that by the end of the chapter, you will too.

After taking a step back from life and looking in, you see that communication is a rather big deal. In business, and in your personal life, you often need to share your ideas with someone. If you can't do this successfully, it can be frustrating for all parties involved.

And it can be costly. Whether pitching to a Venture Capital firm to invest in your company, to expressing why someone should vote you class president, most things in life come down to, as I've coined it, "the pitch and the end-point."

To me, communication is the ability to clearly express my ideas with others around me. It's being able to share my own ideas and have anyone involved understand my intended meaning, in an effective and efficient manner. Good communication skills get results.

It's an idea for a new app you want to create, which has a concept that is intricate and needs to be explained well. A company you want to start with a distinct goal that needs to be heard and understood by others. The completion of a complex math problem, trying to convey to others the steps you took to complete the question. These are all times in which communication skills are crucial in order to share beliefs. In these scenarios, among many others, you are forced to make your 'Pitch' efficiently and effectively so the 'end-point' of the communication shows you and your ideas in a favorable light.

Another important aspect of communication is to be able to actually speak, to not be afraid in group settings, and to contribute to a conversation or lesson appropriately. I can tell you from firsthand experience that in a classroom, 95% of the words spoken come from 25% or less of the students. Many kids in a classroom environment, or even 1-on-1 conversations for that manner, are simply unwilling or unable to contribute in a meaningful way. There is a common fear among many students – it's better to keep ones mouth shut and to say nothing, rather than risk getting the answer wrong. Or worse still, have your classmates laugh at you. It's a sad but true fact.

This is a problem that needs to be solved, because when only a small portion of classmates contributes to the class discussion, the dynamic of the class is skewed, in that a significant portion of the class in underrepresented.

Teachers try to address this problem with class participation, or lack thereof, by assigning a participation grade to students. Now, this encourages *some* students to participate; however, most of the time, it accomplishes very little, because the motivation is too little to allow for change. Which is a shame. Many students would rather accept a poor grade than participate. And many teachers would rather be lenient towards a student's participation grade rather than hand out a grade that is reflective of their actual participation. Which is where the teaching of communication skills comes in.

Incredible communication skills, skills that need to be acquired by all people, especially young people, revolve around the ability to construct an argument based on your own points and make your case clearly so that it has an impact. Whether to a colleague, a boss or to a teacher, everybody should possess the capability to prove their conceptual argument through the proper conveyance of their points.

People of all ages will benefit from improved communication skills. We continually come up with excellent, creative ideas. However, often times, the ideas fall flat and don't succeed due to ineffectual communication in spreading these ideas, which leads to a lack of understanding.

Teaching Communication Skills

Now, in regards to how communication could be taught, I am not recommending it be taught alongside math and science as a full period every day. What I am suggesting is that each day, one full period be devoted to the development of business skills. This is a common program mentioned throughout the book, so pay attention. How this class is structured, what material is taught when, and how much material should be taught in regards to a specific subject is a case-by-case basis, but it is surely important to have a class period every single day that would be dedicated to different business skills.

The communication skills portion of the class should be focused on the following: how to become a more active listener, and how to better convey an idea in a group setting.

To address my plan for implementation, all students need to work to become active listeners. I'll give a bit of my own experiences in this regard.

In a class that my high school created to develop skills among the leaders of the grade, called, 'Peer Educators', a large chunk of the curriculum at the beginning of the year revolved around learning how to become active listeners. This included learning how to express ourselves respectfully but assertively, how to convey ideas in a group setting, and how to be involved in group discussions with appropriate behavior. After this portion of our class was completed, every student had improved their ability to be active listeners.

Here, we could put forward our advice and suggestions in the group setting with respect, and we could be instrumental in having an active and thought-provoking dialogue. This type of curriculum, situational and learning through example, needs to be implemented in the communication portion of the business class. Every person could become infinitely more effective in many types of scenarios through this, especially considering that there are many nuances that need be understood and followed under the premise of communication.

Focus needs to be placed on the meaning of what you wish to communicate, and also paying close attention to what you say and how you say it. Yes, these rules can be read; however, they will be more fully understood and more meaningfully implemented when learned in a classroom environment, through actual hands-on experience, and from group involvement. Implementation of this type of curriculum will encourage the development of more active listeners, and result in a new generation of excellent communicators!

Expert Opinions

Thomas Cormen

Thomas Cormen, a Computer Science Professor at Dartmouth, elaborated on the fact that communication in today's world, especially as it relates to computer science, is extremely important. Mr. Cormen stated that at Dartmouth, he would much rather have a student with knowledge of how to write and read English correctly and how to communicate well with no knowledge of computer science, rather then work with a student who possesses the knowledge of how to write a computer program with no communication skills.

Cormen went on to say that if a student cannot write a clear expository piece, such as the ones that he would students formulate for his classes at Dartmouth, then that student could not succeed where they had hoped to. In his opinion, it is extremely important to communicate effectively with people, as it pays off in every way of life.

Communication is also critical as it pertains to 'wetware'. This is the thought processes that are regarded as analogous to computer systems, more so than with hardware. Cormen believes that communication of ideas and hopes or anything along the line of communication is extremely important in the real world. You need to know how to write well, how to speak well, and how to put together a PowerPoint with proper communication skills.

One must be able to convey their message in a way that makes sense, Cormen explained. Ultimately, he said, all aspects of communication are more important to your career than learning how to handle a computer, even in computer science. Its importance is even more relevant during an age like the one we living in today. Cormen even went as far as to elaborate on personal experiences he has had that help show why communication is so important.

For four years, Thomas Cormen was assigned to be the Director of the Writing program at Dartmouth. At that time, he had to think about what his goal was in that office, and why he wished to accomplish that. It was then he realized something. He mentioned that some of his students at Dartmouth might be writing code and creating computer programs as an engineer over a period of 5 years, but ultimately, the ability to advance their career lay in the key skill of the ability to communicate to people. Just as a relatable-field example, if you have a startup company, for example, you have to communicate your idea to pitch it to investors or potential customers. Even a field as seemingly unrelated as Computer Programming can be tremendously affected by communication.

Communication is an integral part of life and business and such its importance cannot be underestimated.

Robert Marzano

In essence, communication plays a role in all relationship skills. I don't think that comes as a surprise to anyone. However, professional relationships require that people should conduct themselves on a professional level at all times. Remember that a text is the means of communication that is most often misunderstood.

Robert Marzano believes that the art of communication is central to the entirety of Language Arts. Communication itself may be a broad term to use, but communication is important, especially at a conceptual level. Communication is produced by the formation key elements in a presentation. You must find the purpose of what you are trying to communicate, and then understand the environment and context behind that communication.

Conclusion

A simple expression that comes to mind when you think of communication is: Say What You Mean. Sounds simple, doesn't it? Not by a long shot. Communication is a difficult skill to develop and maintain. It cannot neither be bought nor gifted. From my personal experience, I can tell you that not being able to contribute unless thoroughly provoked is a major setback in the world at large, and it needs to stop. It is a shame that so many students feel ill equipped to participate in class discussions.

And those who possess it often enjoy prosperity and happier lives. This is why middle schools should implement the art of communication as part of its curriculum.

CHAPTER 5

Mathematics

D efined as the 'abstract science of number, quantity, and space,' math is an essential component of life. Whether studied as an entity unto itself, or in combination with other subjects such as physics or engineering, it plays an immense role in many aspects of our lives. Due to the all-pervading influence of math, we should change the way the math courses at the middle school level are implemented.

My Perspective On Math

When I think of middle-school math and middle school in general, I believe that a lot of what we learned is not based on any relevancy to everyday in life, or it's value for your future. In fact, I believe this to be true of much that is taught in school.

Overall, teachers only teach what is required to pass the state tests. When I first realized this, I was shocked. Teachers and students both just focus on whatever is on the state test that year. In the minds of teachers, that is all that needs to be taught. And in the mind of students, it's all that needs to be learned. I'll get heavier into state testing throughout the rest of the book, but I'll go a little more into it now.

Depending on the state test that year, mathematics could be very beneficial as a whole to the student body, or it could be a total 'flop' and a complete waste of students' time. All curriculums for math should be taught for the former reason. According to one student, "Almost anything in life is more important than circle math." And you know what, he's not wrong.

In Syosset, where I go to school, the state test for middle school math is the State-Wide Regents Examination. Now, after a few changes from the state, there are now 2 different tests, where the student's higher grade is marked: The Common Core Test and The regular Regents Exam. Various levels of difficulty and topics are covered, and as such, students focus is shifted away from what actually is important in math, to the stricter, less-practical, more-applicable-to-testing side of the subject.

I'm going to make a statement that very few other students will make: I don't mind math. Not at all really. What I didn't like about math, however, was the coursework assigned and the lessons instilled in us during middle school. Due to middle school math, which for me was a combination of boredom and insufficient challenge, I felt that my overall mathematical ability dropped at a steady rate. So, at least for me, middle school math was a big fat joke. I truly believe that my math skills suffered in the long run.

Another major problem I had with middle school math was that it left my classmates and I with a *disconnect* of what was expected to be known and understood in High School. In the end of the day, I was expected to know more than was actually taught. There was a large gap between middle school curriculum and what should've been taught (but it wasn't taught because it wasn't really on state tests), and high school expectation of what should be known. Many of my classmates and I feel that coming into 9th grade after middle school, we were put at a huge disadvantage right off the bat.

Additionally, Middle school math, much like middle school writing, does not validate its material with every passing year. Since this chapter was written on a Thursday, let's take a quick #TBT (or a Throwback Thursday) to Harry B. Thompson Middle School, where my classmates and I started our middle school. I remember vividly one of the very first topics we learned in 6th grade, one that we would come to hate: complicated long division.

Many people find long division an exercise of complete and utter boredom. I had to participate in this mind-numbing skill-that-isn't-really-a-skill very often, and with paper and pencil no less, in order to solve the complicated division equations we were assigned by our teachers. The concept of handwritten math was a major part of that year's curriculum. After all, we were young kids coming out of elementary school.

Hand-written problems were considered the perfect tool for students of that age and intellectual level, right? Well, I beg to differ!

Forget the fact that we spent the better part of a year learning what I believe to be the least important skill ever. Forget the fact that we wasted a large part of the year practicing it, applying it, mastering it, over and over and over again. A very weird concept, yes: Mastering Long Division. What boggles my mind, though, is that the following year after learning this incredibly dull mathematical skill, we find ourselves in 7th grade with a huge change. 7th grade came with exciting new possibilities and the possible expansion of learning and knowledge, especially considering that *you get to use a calculator!* Yes, you get to utilize a plastic rectangular device that helps solve problems efficiently and effectively. It's a miracle! No more long division. Just 'plug and chug', as my 10th grade math teacher likes to say.

With the utilization of a calculator comes a shocking realization: you realize that the entirety of what one learned in 6th grade is entirely obsolete. Outdated, archaic, superseded and outmoded. Well at least that is how it feels. It invokes feelings of incredible annoyance, and irritation. There is no pain, no disappointment - it just makes you think all the hard work you put in prior year turned out to be a waste of time, because you get a calculator with a forward-slash symbol on it.

Schoolteachers, administrators, and policy-makers alike managed to waste an entire grade of arguably the most important subject in school by giving us a calculator. Is there anything more demeaning than a giant waste of time? Imagine you had been developing certain skills in an attempt to accomplishing a goal. Then when you get to a certain point on your journey, you realize that it has all been for nothing. This perfectly summarizes what my peers and I feel: disgust! Oh, and if only it ended there, I wouldn't have bothered to make a stink about it, but that's not all.

Now, let's move on for the second example. A large component of 7th grade mathematics revolved around graphing. How to make graphs, how to solve graphs, how to interpret graphs. Many months were spent mastering these concepts. Students were given the tasks of utilizing equations of lines and circles and plotting points by hand. We had to take all of our hand-drawn diagrams, and solve and interpret them to the best of our abilities, pertaining to the questions at hand. Boring, definitely, but an exercise that could play an important role down the road, right? WRONG.

At the end of 7th grade, each student received the next step up in math: Graphing Calculators! Yet again a full year of math turned on its head, becoming almost as antiquated as long division. Another huge disappointment.

It's an outrageous concept, right? The fact is that each grade in middle school basically made the prior year useless in math, with the help of pre-existing technology!

With each grade invalidating the one before it, there is simply no point in learning any of this material. Reflecting upon it now, all of the curriculum 'taught' in 6th and 7th grade could have easily been replaced with less than a month of teaching on how to use our TI-issued calculators properly, even by teaching shortly how to do it by hand and explaining the concepts at hand. Students also could have benefited from being taught all the cool tricks and functions that no one would discover on their own, as a result of extra time. Here, student's time and hard work would not have been wasted.

We could then have focused on more important tasks and ideas. Two entire years of schooling for a full subject should not be wasted. This is why we need to change the way math is taught in middle schools.

Computer Programming and Applied Mathematics

One thing that some students would like to see incorporated into math class, and which has a chapter of its own later on, is a few classes in basic computer programming. These are the languages and techniques used to create websites, program computers, and make other types of software and hardware programs. One student said that these types of lessons might help students uncover a passion for computer programming, which could lead to a career somewhere down the road. In fact, many of my contemporaries have discovered a passion for computer coding, and wish to continue their learning, as the result of exposure.

These lessons would be much different from the standard practices of teaching. They would provide unconventionality yet simplicity in the teachings of smaller things, such as logic (which also has its own chapter later on). Implementation of a side-course in the math classroom may take some doing, yes, because of the many rules and regulations with regards to schools, curriculum and testing, but it's most certainly worth a try.

A 'new-school' approach to teaching and implementing computer code would make lessons more beneficial for students. It creates new focus and gives kids new opportunities, Personally, I am only just beginning to learn computer programming and I am absolutely fascinated by it. I am so captivated, that in fact, it may be one of the career paths I choose to pursue later in life. If only I had found out about this revolutionary pathway for success earlier, my possibilities would've been endless. As stated by one student, a programmer who now is creating software for the high-end shoe market, who was introduced to code in early middle school, "It was the best choice I ever made. It allows me almost unlimited possibilities, and I really do enjoy it."

Isn't this the point of school? To be able to find what excites you and take advantage of it? Unfortunately, for most students, this is rarely the case.

Now, yes, many students might find computer programing boring and unimaginative. Likewise, some people enjoy watching men's figure skating, others don't. There are many units in school where some students are captivated and others are not. Teaching a few basic lessons on the ideologies and concepts of programming could help a few kids in the long run. This is more of a "Tidbit Unit", a trailer if you will. It teases kids and excites them enough that they want more.

Practical Mathematics

One thing that Middle School definitely should have taught was Practical Math. This is math that you would need daily, rather than the stuff that only applies if you're an architect or engineer; it's quick math that comes up in your everyday life, revolving around quick uses of simple skills in math overall. Practical math has applications to everyday life, and is invaluable. For example, it's being able to do the quick math in your head when looking at a sale. Can you tell me what 40%

off of a $20 shirt is? What about needing to use a tip calculator app at a restaurant to properly tip your waiter?

In my town, it's a rare sight to see an adult calculating what 15% of the bill should be for the tip without using a calculator. After all, most people consider this type of practical math to be difficult.

In reality, it's rather simple to do. My father explained to me how to do this math for the first time when I was about 8, and it was always revolved around finding simple tricks. For instance, he showed me that to calculate 15% of the bill at a restaurant, all you have to do is take 1/10 of the total by moving the decimal point over one place to the left. Then take half of that number. Add the two values together, and you get 15% of whatever your bill may be.

Simple tricks and tools such as the one above clearly demonstrate the need for teaching practical math, in order to ensure every student coming out of middle school is not coming out with a disadvantage.

My Dream for Applied Mathematics

Every student I interviewed said they wanted to know more practical math, plain and simple.

This type of math is barely touched upon in school, and even if it is, teachers and curriculum makers didn't do a very good job, as no one remembers it. When I shared the "tip calculation tip" with a fellow student, he remarked, "This stuff is actually practical and cool, and I really need this. It's the first piece of math I might be able to use." Everyone, young and old, needs to know more practical math. It should be discussed more in-depth school, as opposed to being taught quickly and treated as though it wasn't important.

'Life Math' is also important because it will help you later in life no matter who you are. It is necessary for all types of jobs, and it can be useful in social settings. When you go out to dinner with your friends, you don't want to have to ask them how to calculate 15% for the tip, or how much you're saving when utilizing a 30% off coupon. This would embarrass most people. It could be so easily avoided, just by being taught practical math rather than long division.

Early middle school provides the perfect outlet in which practical math can be taught. This is especially because courses taught later on in middle school are generally the foundation for high school, so it's best to deviate and teach applied math early in middle school, and change the way we live.

Expert Opinions

Deborah Meier

Deborah Meier believes that the biggest concern regarding mathematics in middle schools is the reliance on utilization of technology, specifically as it relates to teaching and learning a certain topic. She believes that utilizing technology when learning a new topic skips over students actually understanding what they are doing, so that they end up mindlessly pressing buttons on your calculator, instead of understanding the math and reasoning behind it. Meier believes that it is very important that a heavier focus should be placed on the underlying structure of mathematics, rather than focusing on the "mechanical" side of mathematics (punching in buttons on your calculator). This would help combat the problem of not understanding what you are doing in the classroom.

Now, this belief is perfectly in line with my theories, but it might not seem so.

The main problem of contradiction arises with Ms. Meier saying we need to understand the underlying principles of mathematics without the use of technology. I stated that it was not wise to learn the topics and then make them obsolete a year later. However, the two are very similar. I believe, very simply, that the use of technology should only *supplement* the remaining curriculum associated with one subject. I believe that the two should be used in unison to create the best possible learning experience for the student, rather than learning by hand in one grade and then learning to use a calculator to perform the same task in the grade that follows. Working in unison is always better than working in confliction.

I am an incredibly big believer that every student has to have an understanding about what they're doing. It needs to make sense for them. They need to know *why* they are doing what they do, *what* it can be used for, and calculations should be practiced both by hand and through the facilitation of technology, just with more time spent with technology, especially after the initial stages of the lesson.

I am also a big believer that students should not have to spend an extended period of time studying the subject and working on that topic by hand, which often seems to be a waste of time. If one could cut the period of time that for learning how to do Topic A in half, you could accomplish so much more within the curriculum. For example, you could take this time and explain what the lesson is accomplishing in regards to what it has to do in the grand scheme of math, what it has to do in relation to other concepts, and where you would use this math outside the classroom. By providing the student with a big picture of the math at hand, they would have a greater understanding of math in general. Overall, this works out greatly for important time allotments in school.

One thing I've come to learn now is that not everything has to be done by hand. For instance, instead of making the students do Applications 1, 2, and 3 within Topic A by hand, you could just have them do Application 1, and then supplement 2 and 3 with the assistance of technology. This allows for maximum efficiency and increased learning. Without providing them that understanding, you greatly devalue that student's shot of *mastering* the material at hand. And it also saves time!

I remember once in math, I was so confused because of the fact during one unit, such little time was used to answer the questions that should be answered during class (because we were doing everything by hand, which took forever). I was so confused; one day, I resorted to going to my older brother, who had to explain to me why I was learning a math concept. He then gave me the big picture. From this, I was able to understand so much more than I thought possible on the subject, and realized that all students should experience a sense of knowledge like that on every topic in math.

Meier completely scribes to the same school of thought. She found that when kids who learned solely with the benefit of technology were given problems to do by hand, they were completely lost. They had no concept or understanding of the methods used to arrive at a solution. They were just used to plugging away at a calculator. They didn't have the basic knowledge or understanding to solve the problems at hand. Calculators make life easier, but kids should always understand the basic principles of mathematics regardless.

Also, one thing that really stuck me after interviewing Meier, which she also brought up heavily, was how much importance in mathematics is placed solely on getting the correct answer, rather than on the creative aspect of problem solving. This is important for a variety of reasons.

For example, let's start with the fact that it puts less pressure on kids to get everything right all the time! From firsthand experience, I can tell you that it gets very scary when all you have to worry about on a test is getting a right answer, such as on a multiple-choice state test. With such heavy importance placed on obtaining the correct results, students only want to solve the problem, not show work or care about how they solved the problem, or the thinking behind solving this problem. This just sets up many bad habits for later down the road, because when you don't care about the journey, then you never get to the desired endpoint.

Obviously not all tests are like this. Some teachers and exams do place some importance on the process of solving the problem. After all, math in its most basic state is problem solving, and solving problems is paramount to success in life.

Regardless, curriculum must be tailored to ensure that heavy emphasis is shown on the way to get to the answer, as opposed to the answer itself.

Robert Marzano

Robert Marzano also had something else to say on the subject. Marzano, an educational expert, began our interview with a brief history of math education, which I think is worth sharing. Apparently, years ago, math study was entirely focused on algorithms. An algorithm is a process or set of rules that are to be followed strictly in calculations or other problem-solving operations. At this time, students were told to memorize specific 'math facts' and processes. However, this style of math can only take one so far in life.

Marzano believes a key element that should be incorporated in math curriculums is the concept of *mathematical thinking*. This is not the memorization of formulas and other related parts of math, but rather the ability to communicate both on paper and verbally, in possessing a conceptual understanding. Whether referring to basic things like multiplication and division, or more complex subject matter like factoring quadratic equations, more emphasis should be placed on how to find the answer, not just the solution.

When Marzano was in high school, he went through the dreaded mathematics curriculum I spoke of earlier. He was taught to memorize algorithms, such as the algorithm for long division. He found that this conventional method of learning is not the type of education that should be placed in curriculums today. Instead, the focus should be on understanding what you are learning on a deeper level.

Rather than this, students should focus on the concepts of functions in math class, and how the functions are represented by different equations. They should also focus on how the variables and constants involved in what's in front of you interact, especially associated with models. He says how this is a prime instance where the important concepts necessary for mathematical success are discussed, in which a conceptual understanding of functions could and should be divided from classes.

This is especially important as this can manifest in many different ways. From physics to biology to psychology, all different walks of life involve variables and the need to understand their interaction, ranging from human interaction to particle reaction to emotional reaction. Learning to think at a conceptual level and practice doing it, as opposed to memorizing algorithms and formulas, could truly benefit students. Again, thinking about these relationships between variables, with certain types of dependencies and results, is all part of implementation in later life.

In addition, utilizing the concepts of functions, you can find examples in the real world that relate to the students, making class so much better. I can tell you that one of the best lessons I've ever had was when in science, we were learning about the interaction of substances, and our teacher really showed us by taking us outside and doing appropriate experiments. He lit fires, he combined chemicals; it was so cool! And the best part? I learned more from that lesson than I would have from reading the textbook chapter 10 times. Let's just say I did really well on that test.

Anyways, these functions in the real world are great examples of real-life problem solving. With the concepts of functions taught and applied in middle school math class, you can also obtain the actual equation that represents that function, which continues to help fuel the perusal of realistic mathematics. Talk about a possible plus for teachers and students alike.

Let's use the concept of football here. In football, a major category of statistics for the Quarterback (aka the QB), involves his QB Rating. Now, QB ratings are a prime example of real life math that gives students the opportunity to find examples of *polynomials* being used in everyday life. Every QB Rating can be represented by a polynomial to determine an end result, which are each different in their own way. Also, something you may not have known is that the polynomial for professional football QB ratings differs from the polynomial utilized in college football QB ratings. To summarize, different categories are worth different amounts in different levels, which could impact a QB's statistical performance, and this perfectly displays real-world math at its finest (at least to most guys).

This is an example Marzano presented to me, one that I myself was unaware of, and it is one that I feel I strongly connected to and one I believe many people will understand and relate to well. The applications of functions for real life are direct examples of the manipulation and creation of conceptualities learned in school with added student interest. When students start to apply these concepts, they can start to see things as mathematical representations in the real world. When I personally experience this, I feel I gain an infinitely greater understanding. This type of interaction has worked for mathematicians throughout history, from the past to the present, and I believe it will work now.

Marzano writes that this is the focus of education going forward; a curriculum entailing what he hopes education takes a turn for, and he writes that hopefully all textbooks take a shorter time to catch up to the current material at hand.

Overall, I 100% agree with Marzano and his beliefs and our hope-to-be plan for education.

Robert Goodman

Robert Goodman is the Executive Director for the Center for Teaching and Learning, an organization whose mission, "is to empower teachers to be leaders in the transformation of public schools so that all students have access to a high-quality education." In short, he knows a lot about education, and showed it in bringing about an interesting way of teaching Math in grades K-12.

Goodman suggested implementing the 'Round Table Method' in math, which entails a group classroom environment, a setting in which he feels people work their absolute best. In this environment, Goodman said he would put together a program revolving around the basic idea of *teaching first* and then *learning second* (yes, there is a difference). Here, Goodman says that the teacher would demonstrate the material at hand, and keep the material limited to a short amount of time, such as 5 to 10 minutes. This is to prevent both the rambling of teachers and the boredom of students.

Goodman then recommends that the teacher follow up the demonstration by posing a problem or challenge to their students. Whether it is a brief problem spanning 1 minute of work or a complex, multi-step problem requiring 20 minutes of intense work, students in class need to be given a problem to solve in order to reaffirm their knowledge of the material. Here, Goodman elaborates, groups of kids would work at round tables (used for the easy ability to talk and discuss with all sitting at the table), talk the problem through (talking about what parts need to be done, which approach to take, just to name a few), and finally solve the equation, as well add new ideas and their own abilities in regards to building off past lessons.

The students would not just be given a simple 'use formula x to get answer y'. Rather, students, in groups of 3, for example, would spend time trying to use their existing knowledge, the information presented at the lesson that day, and the utilization of critical thinking in order to solve complex questions.

These groups would then demonstrate their accomplishments; they would share their ideas with the class, so everyone else can see that team's solution and the steps of how to obtain that answer, and all other ideas associated with that problem. Now, Goodman admits that the class might have many different solutions among themselves, which is fine, considering that students should then begin to discuss and use logical thinking to uncover the proper answer. During the discussion, a series of different problems along the same lines can be built upon to learn and understand the best ideas and practices.

I completely agree with this approach. I know that if they had this at my middle school, I surely would have flourished the way that this ideology allows for. This type of setup, which can be used for lessons involving the simplest reading of a clock to the hardest AP Calculus lesson, allows for a scaffolding of problems that can be used to understand each part of the topic at hand. This further entails students understanding every concept pertaining to that one topic. One can then branch off into new long-term projects or other questions that require logical thinking combined with knowledge of that lesson.

All in all, Goodman brings to the table one heck of an idea. It is both spectacular in its simplicity yet marvelous in its own complexities.

David Warlick

David Warlick also had an excellent point to make on the subject. Warlick is referred to as "an educator, author, programmer and public speaker... [And] an early adopter and promoter of technology in the classroom." He's someone with a heavy technical background.

When asked about his thoughts on math curriculum, Warlick chose to talk about programming. "If I had my choice, I would teach programming. When you are programming, you are not simply learning Math, you are using Math to work the numbers. You are not trying to find the answer. You are trying the work the numbers in order to produce the answer that you need, in order to make the computer perform the way that you want it to. After my first afternoon of teaching myself how to program, I got on my knees and thanked every algebra teacher I had ever had. It all suddenly made sense."

Besides computer programming, Warlick also wrote about the importance of Statistics in regards to math. "Algebra and Geometry are fine. They help you learn how to think logically. But statistics is about measuring and understanding our world and ourselves. It's critical in an information-abundant time."

Warlick understands the need for learning what is important today, and I feel he touched on the most important changes that need to be made in math, especially in regards to with computer programming.

Conclusion

My father has always said: "People can always tell how smart you are by seeing how good you are at math." Imagine the leg up each and every student could have down the road if the math courses implemented at the middle school level were altered in such a way that students would be well prepared for their future. What a great idea! The craziest part, though, is that it's all possible, and it's not even very difficult to attain. So, why can't we change middle school math for the better?

CHAPTER 6

Financial Literacy

F inancial literacy is said to be the ability to understand how money works in the world. How someone makes money, how that person manages their funds, how they invest their capital, how that person donates the proceeds. The list goes on and on, but this is enough to give you a solid foundation of the concepts we'll be covering this chapter.

Introduction

Financial literacy should be considered an essential skill, one that is required in everyday life. Money is considered to be one of the most important things in any person's life to live, to succeed, and to give back. So, with this, you would think that with financial literacy, being such an invaluable and important skill to have, would have a heavy premium placed on its learning. And here, you would naturally be wrong; that is not the case in middle schools. It's my belief that middle school should be where the introduction to financial knowledge should begin. However, it was certainly not taught in my school, and I definitely believe it should be in the future.

One simple reason why financial literacy should be taught is because as a young adult, it is incredibly important to have a solid foundation in finance. It is something you really need to know these days. It is not an option; in today's world, everyone, regardless of age or gender, should understand basic financial transactions.

A perfect example to supporting this is the group of today's young adults (I mean those in their late teens – early 20s). I could swamp you with an extensive list of facts and properties of financial literacy and statistics, but I'd much rather take a look at the fact that a lot of kids in today's world simply don't know anything about their financial state, or how to handle their assets. I know I personally have a terrible sense of financial literacy; I could never tell you how to balance a checkbook or how to pay bills, not in a million years. When I get married, I hope my spouse knows what's going on in that department; otherwise, we'll be bankrupt quicker than tickets sell out for a Justin Bieber concert. To be perfectly honest, I didn't have a firm grasp of the economy until very recently, simply because it's one of those subjects that's never even mentioned in middle school, and I believe that this has put me at a disadvantage.

Many people find personal finance a challenge. It is a topic that is treated lightly in school, if at all. Even some of the most book smart kids don't know how to manage their money. When 21-year-old college student moves away from home, and they are living on their own for the first time, there is a good chance that their finances are in a terrible state.

An essential part of life for these young adults necessitates having the ability to manage their money. Yet many are unable to do so. And this Mismanagement and fiscal irresponsibility often translates to debt. One student interviewed for this book told a personal story about a sibling living under these exact circumstances. Financial distress as a result of lack of knowledge and experience is all around us, and it's not going to improve unless we make a change. The bottom line is this: kids in the 21st century are entering the work force and are not properly prepared for what awaits them. That's why financial literacy needs to be taught.

I read this great article also about why Financial Literacy is important from bbt.com, different from my own beliefs I just shared, and thought I should share it:

"...Making thoughtful and informed decisions about your finances is more important than ever. Several trends are converging that demonstrate the importance of financial literacy:

More and more, the burden of making sound financial decisions is coming to rest on the shoulders of consumers. Many companies have shifted their retirement plans from traditional pension plans to those requiring employees to participate in, pay part of the cost for, and make investment decisions about. 401(k) plans are the best example of this.

Social Security used to be seen as a major source, if not the major source, of retirement income. Now it serves more like a safety net that will provide enough only for survival, not enjoyment.

We are living longer. This means that we must have accumulated more funds before retirement to cover living expenses over a longer time. Otherwise, we could become a burden for our families.

The financial environment seems like it is changing faster. Bull markets, bear markets, rising interest rates, falling interest rates, and the increased number of finance-related articles with conflicting views in the press can make creating and following a financial path difficult.

There are more financial options. Hundreds of credit card options, several types of mortgages, different types of IRAs, and the ever-growing number of investment options further complicate financial decision making.

There are more choices of financial services companies. Banks, credit unions, brokerage firms, insurance firms, credit card companies, mortgage companies, financial planners, and others are all trying to get your business.

The numbers themselves seem to have gotten larger. Costs and wages have generally continued to rise to the point where having an income or retirement nest egg that several years ago would have seemed luxurious, now just seems barely adequate."

This is an excellent article in my opinion, providing fresh insight as to the need for financial literacy.

Teaching Financial Literacy in School

Financial Literacy should be a mandatory class in middle schools, as part of the one-period per-day rotating class that I envision will be the most important innovation in schooling since the invention of Spark Notes. I believe that it would be invaluable, particularly if taught in middle schools. After all, our financial futures depend on it! Also, these middle schools provide the perfect platform to learn financial literacy. One student said it best, in that, "There are so many unimportant classes that seem irrelevant, that at least one mandatory class that would benefit everyone equally, unlike every other required class, would be so beneficial." And I agree.

On that note, I would like to share another excerpt from an article from investopedia.com; an excellent read if I do say so, about the need for financial literacy:

"[In today's world] Banks and other institutions are inundating consumers with credit opportunities—the ability to apply for credit cards or use credit checks to pay other credit balances—and without the proper knowledge or checks and balances, it is easy to get into financial trouble. In past generations, cash was used for virtually every purchase. Today, cash is rarely used. The way we shop has changed as well. Online shopping has become the top choice for many younger shoppers, creating ample opportunities to use and overextend credit, an all too easy way to accumulate debt, fast. Many of these consumers have very little understanding of finances, how credit works and the potential impact on their financial well-being for many, many years. In fact, the lack of financial understanding has been signaled as one of the main reasons behind savings and investing problems faced by many Americans.

Financial literacy is the confluence of financial, credit and debt management and the knowledge that is necessary to make financially responsible decisions—decisions that are integral to our everyday lives. Financial literacy includes understanding how a checking account works, what using a credit card really means, and how to avoid debt. In sum, financial literacy impacts the daily decisions an average family makes when trying to balance a budget, buy a home, fund their children's education and ensure an income at retirement.

A lack of financial literacy is not a problem only in emerging or developing economies. Consumers in developed or advanced economies also fail to demonstrate a strong grasp of financial principles in order to understand and negotiate the financial landscape, manage financial risks effectively and avoid financial pitfalls. Nations globally, from Korea to Australia, or from Germany to the U.S., are faced with populations who do not understand financial basics...

The level of financial literacy varies according to education and income levels, but evidence shows that highly educated consumers with high incomes can be just as ignorant about financial issues as less educated, lower income consumers. [It's especially important to teach financial literacy in schools, to equalize any disadvantage for those in lower income households who may not otherwise have access to this information]. And it seems consumers are hesitant to learn. The Organization for Economic Co-operation and Development (OECD) cited a survey conducted in Canada which found choosing the right investment for a retirement savings plan was more stressful than a visit to the dentist...

Financial literacy is crucial to help ensure consumers save enough to provide adequate income in retirement while avoiding high levels of debt that might result in bankruptcy and foreclosures. A study from financial services company TIAA-CREF showed that those with high financial literacy plan for retirement and in essence have double the wealth of people who do not plan for retirement. Conversely, those with low financial literacy borrow more, have less wealth and end up paying unnecessary fees for financial products. In other words, those with lower financial literacy tend to buy on credit, and are unable to pay their full balance each month and end up spending more on interest fees. This group also does not invest, has trouble with debt and a poor understanding of the terms of their mortgages or loans. Even more worrisome, many consumers believe that they are far more financially literate than they really are.

And while this may seem like an individual problem, it is broader in nature and more influential on the entire population than previously believed. All one needs to do is look at the financial crisis of 2008 to see the financial impact on the entire economy from a lack of understanding of mortgage products and the subsequent defaults. Financial literacy is an issue with broad implications for economic health and an improvement can lead the way to a global economy that is competitive and strong."

This was a very comprehensive and well-written piece about financial literacy in totality; one that I feel also perfectly exemplifies the nature of financial literacy.

So, how many adults have difficulty managing taxes, handling student loans, allocating money, etc.? The answer is more than you might think. Sad, yes, but true.

Making a Change

To combat money mismanagement, change needs to be implemented. Financial literacy should be taught under a specific curriculum as part of my mandatory period program. This mandated financial management curriculum would teach students about taxes, student loans, how to balance a checkbook, and all of the other *important and real life concepts* associated with basic finance. Now, of course, no one is going to become a financial genius in one day; this is why a gradual program such as the one exhibited here will teach the basics that need to be implemented. As an overview, I view this opportunity for financial literacy as an introductory course that will prepare you for your future over a period of 1-2 years as a part of the entire curriculum. I am suggesting dedicating one period a day to the development of life skills to prepare us for our future.

The same article quoted earlier, from bbt.com, also went on to give great tips for simple things that can be used to "reduce financial anxiety", which I feel apply for being financially literate and making a change:

"Be as informed as you can be about your finances. After all, you are the one who is going to have to live with your decisions.

Try to find a financial institution or financial advisor that is knowledgeable, that you can trust, and with whom you can work comfortably. They cannot make all your decisions, but they should be able to help you put your situation into perspective and help you evaluate your options.

Try to develop good financial habits. Just paying attention to how you spend your money will probably lead to some ideas about how to save more. Over time, your savings can make a large difference in your future financial lifestyle.

Do the easy things. Participating in your company's retirement plan, contributing to an IRA, starting to save early for a college education, enrolling for direct deposit of your paycheck, and using some form of automatic saving plan will help you accumulate funds. In addition, you will know you are taking positive actions.

Try to develop a financial plan of some sort. It does not have to be complicated or extensive. In fact, you may want to tackle one part of your finances at a time, such as looking at all your insurance needs. Breaking up a financial plan into smaller, workable pieces can make it easier to create."

I really feel that these simple tips from bbt.com are really helpful, and even though they don't go into great detail, it's a great piece nonetheless.

Financial Goals and Lifestyle

To further delve into my plan for increasing financial knowledge among primary school students, another important aspect of financial literacy that needs to be taught ties into lifestyle and goals. One important concept regarding the topic of financial literacy involves the difference between *lifestyle goals* and *financial goals*. Now, prior to taking a Massive Open Online Course (aka MOOC) on the subject, I thought the two were one and the same. How wrong I was! I had no idea that lifestyle and your finances, not vice versa, control lifestyle goals. I had no idea that financial goals dictate your lifestyle, and in fact influence your entire life; supposedly, they should be the most important factor in almost every decision you make. Who thought goal setting was so important? I didn't, but I do realize it now.

Also, the entire concept of the stock market and investing were very poorly explained to me as a student. I believe understanding these concepts to be valuable beyond measure for a young teenager. To give some background, as an 8th grader in my middle school, there was an additional period embedded into our schedule, that could be used for either taking a full 1-year research class or taking two half-year courses of either Home Ed., Technology, and Business. I chose to take the

Business and Technology courses, and below I'll talk about my experiences with the Business course.

The Stock Market Game

I was very excited about my new business class. My brothers always knew so much about business and investing, and I was excited at the opportunity to gain the same knowledge; I looked forward to having intellectual conversations on the subject with them and my father. I expected a very serious, detailed, and highly informative course.

However, instead of the course I envisioned in my mind, I was met with a poor curriculum that basically consisted of playing the Stock Market Game with a randomly assigned group of kids. Throughout the class for half the year, the stock market and principles of finance had not been properly explained nor understood. Unfortunately, from day one of that class, I could tell that I had already knew more about business than I was going to learn during the entire class.

To summarize, Finance was not well explained, and the class turned the Stock Market Game into a guessing game. We watched Squawk Box and purchased highlighted stocks and sold as a guessing game based on random or cool acronyms. And from what I understand, this is a prevalent occurrence at other schools as well.

This is a shame; one should not complete a business course and still have no knowledge of business and the stock market. I came out of a class centered in stocks, not knowing how the price of a stock was calculated. I did not even learn how stocks were purchased in real life. How can anyone discover a passion for anything if they are not made aware of its existence?

To pursue a passion, you must first be introduced to it! This is a common theme throughout this book, and at the risk of repeating myself, students, especially at the peak age of late middle school and emerging high school, need to be provided with all the tools necessary in order to find what they love and pursue it. And, for me, finance happens to fit this bill quite nicely.

Discovering an Interest In Finance

Many of my close friends who had initially been pushed into taking business or finance courses by their parents came out actually wanting to pursue careers or hobbies in finance.

I'll give a specific example. One of my very close friends recently went through this change in his life. His father, who is heavily involved in the field of economics, decided to educate his son about the stock market by providing him with a special shared account and some funding, where he couldn't actually do anything himself, but rather just told his dad what to do and watched. Through this, my friend was able to experiment with the stock market, research on his own, and most of all, learn through experience.

Today, he is a 16-year-old financial whiz kid, with so much knowledge about the market and understands all other nuances of finance that I only wish I knew! And again, I'm not saying every kid should have access to his or her own private funds, or even joint accounts, (with their parents actually controlling their accounts of course, and executing all associated under their own influence, in order to be legal). Even if all kids just played the Stock Market Game, and took it seriously, with lessons throughout, it would be infinitely more beneficial to the student than learning in some book or playing a guessing game.

Imagine if all middle school students graduated with this knowledge. Think of the implications! The stock market would have an incredible surge in trades, considering kids would be begging their parents to execute the desired trades for them. Knowledge and participation in fields involving finance and economics would skyrocket. Overall, increased knowledge would lead to greater participation and a ripple effect would be the outcome!

Learning to Save and Scams

Another aspect of finance that should be taught in economics is the concept of savings. One life lesson that has been instilled in me from a young age is that when you make any money, you put some away for a rainy day. From personal experience, this little piece of advice could be the difference between food on your plate and a moving sign on your front lawn, especially considering the tumultuous economies in the world we live in. Saving for the future is an extremely important concept in life, yet I don't know the first thing about it!

I've been told numerous times by my family that, "In later life you have to construct a savings plan that factors in your income and the entirety of your expenses in order to further establish a fallback plan in life, and that further you could use that savings plan to facilitate the risks associated with today's market and economy and can further assist you in achieving personal goals in the field of finance, which in turn helps adjust to better your lifestyle goals." That sounds like a whole lot, but it is something that could easily be covered in a simple financial course.

A few more instrumental parts of finance that everyone should understand in today's world include How compound interest works, The basic risks involved with debt, asset classes, and my favorite, How to identify and avoid financial scams. I favor this principle of finance, because I only realized it as a part of economics very recently.

In matter of fact, a few weeks before writing this chapter, I read an article, which featured a spam email reading the following that I knew I had to include (verbatim):

Please read this is not spaM

Hey its Dee Dee. I have been traveling abroad with some friends and it looks like my passport, wallet, and dragons have been stolen. I need $520, a ship, and my dragons to get back home.

I know we don't know each other well but if you could please help me I promise I will pay you back and make you a High Lord of the Seven Kingdoms ASAP, as soon as I get back! So sorry I know this is so embarrassing.

Please send money quickly and especially the dragons, because as I said someone has stolen my dragons. They are just gone. The cages are still there but the dragons aren't in them. Also my passport and wallet.

Thanks so much im so sorry and I really appreciate it,

-Daemrys "Dee Dee" Targaryen

Funny, right?

This is just one of the many different types of scam emails you might receive in your inbox one day. The only thing you have to remember here is that any suspicious email needs to be disregarded entirely.

Conclusion

When asked to rate their level of financial literacy, most students interviewed for this book responded with a score of either 2 or 3, with 10 being the most and 1 being the least. If our youth is not financially literate, how can they succeed? Of all the classes in middle school, this would be one that could end up changing someone's life. One student commented, "I'm really worried [about the fact I am not well versed in Finance]. I know how to do the Pythagorean theorem, but shouldn't I also know how to balance a checkbook?"

If financial literacy was taught to young teenagers, then imagine the possibilities for the future. If all American teenagers received a proper introduction to finance, and had the knowledge necessary to make informed decisions and opinions on the subject, then the economy would most certainly be better off.

To wrap up, you know that there has to be a problem when even Ivy League graduates are failing to succeed due to fiscal irresponsibility and lack of financial knowledge. A simple course would give middle school students this invaluable skill of financial literacy for the rest of their lives. And financial literacy is just one example of a business skill that is necessary in the real world today, and which can be easily taught. Let's implement financial literacy in middle schools!

CHAPTER 6

Logic

I magine all of the situations in life where challenges await. Everything from a basketball game to a debate match. Any sport, competition, or test of any kind involves competing with some degree of difficulty to obtain a specific objective. In a basketball game, it's overcoming your opposition by playing strong defense and scoring more points. In a debate match, it's about overcoming the opposition's argument and squashing it like a bug, thereby allowing your arguments and your abilities to shine. In my opinion, the biggest challenge in school does not come in a tangible form, but rather in the form of logic – or the lack of.

My Take On Logic

To me, logic is the critical thinking that is desired and required in most avenues of life. It is the ability to make the best decisions in the face of challenges and options. It is about *choices*. It's being able to overcome difficulty through the application of one's skills in a manner that allows you to gain the upper hand.

Logic is so important to me, and plays an important role in my life. This is because the use of logic creates options and opportunity, and as a 15-year-old, that's not something you hear very often. Through logic, students can make the best possible choices of any number of different routes to take, in any application. If logic were taught in middle school, then more kids would understand and believe they have greater choice and greater opportunity in a large number of situations.

High School requires using logic in order to solve a myriad of problems. Word problems need to be examined and analyzed, other math problems need to be assessed and the appropriate formula applied; in many ways, math revolves around the utilization of Logic. The part-skill, part practice-makes-perfect *tool* is defined as 'the science that involves a proper or reasonable way of thinking about or understanding a concept'. This can be said in order to succeed in math as well as in regards to problem solving. After all, as it relates to all work, logic is very important.

When I was in the 9th grade, I can you that the degree of logic involved with that math curriculum was very extensive, and required much implementation; as such, it should have been discussed and built upon in middle school. As a graduate of the standard middle school curriculum, the adjustment to an incredibly logic-based informational system was a difficult transition. I was ill prepared and so were many of my classmates, who regarded this lack of logical ability to be the biggest academic disconnect they ever faced.

Is this a bold and credible claim by others and myself? Absolutely. In my mind, logic is one of the most difficult ideologies yet one of the most practical tools utilized for a student at any age. Logic is not something that can be written down in a textbook, or presented as a set of instructions on a worksheet. It is undoubtedly the most complex and advanced skill. Because of the fact that logic cannot be written down in formula form and spoon-fed to students, *it simply cannot be taught*.

A **bold** statement indeed (get it?). But it's true. In my opinion, through my experiences in life, in both real-world situations and classroom settings, logic is something that cannot be taught. Problem solving cannot be taught.

Now, some of you may beg to differ. However, what sets me apart from my contemporaries and their statements of, "even if it is true, what are you going to do about it?" is that I have a solution. Logic cannot be taught, no. But it is an ideology at its core, and as such, it can be *reinforced*.

Logic is a skill that is only obtained through constant practice requiring its use, and as such, a good idea to reinforce logical thinking is by frequently being given small "tests" – not actual paper tests, but rather the occasional question that requires problem solving here and there to gauge understanding.

But even then, logic is not inherent in all kids. Some people are simply more logical than others. It is of little consequence because one trait will not make or break an entire person's life. We are a society of many people with many talents.

My 'Success' Story

I would like to share a personal story of my "successes". For the majority of my 9th grade school year, I was fortunate enough to have the opportunity to be exposed to the world of logic and problem solving. When I say this, I mean applying logical techniques to solve a given task. After my older brother, Justin, came up with the idea of hosting a conference for Millennials about Entrepreneurship, I jumped at the opportunity, helping him wherever I could.

My initial tasks were the equivalent to taking a dive into the deep end of the adult pool, in that I had to obtain sponsors for my brother's conference. Now, imagine a young, somewhat immature, a tad cocky, but above all youthful kid attempting to make a play in a world that most adults fail to succeed. Not looking too good, right?

Nonetheless, I carried on with my duties for the conference. It was my hope that I could do a good job and prove the disbelievers wrong. I wanted to prove that even though I was young, I could do it. However, I had to answer the biggest question I had ever encountered to this day: "How do I succeed where others have failed?" I brainstormed for hours, sent hundreds of emails, and drove myself nuts searching the Internet for potential companies. I spent hours scouring other conferences to see what they did. This is what required logic, in that I had to problem solve to figure out how to succeed.

The result? I undoubtedly, totally FAILED. Yep, that's right. I didn't nail a single sponsor. I let my brother down (sorry bro), and I proved everyone right.

But, upon reflection, it was one of the greatest things I could have ever done. I was transformed from a youthful-minded kid to a mature young adult. That's because while I failed in obtaining sponsors, I gained in problem-solving abilities.

It was absolutely incredible, how I could fail so completely and yet accomplish so much. But it's true. I learned how to hunt down companies, how to find companies that would even consider sponsoring, how to cold email the right way. Yes, I had failed in the traditional sense. But the fact that at 14 years of age, I had the ability to take such a challenging and perplexing problem and turn it a lesson in problem solving was incredible.

Moving forward, I was able to overcome being somewhat scared of the real world, becoming someone who could figure things out for myself. And because I tried to do something and had total success (again, not "real" success in my designated task, but rather a success in an underlying way), I encourage everyone to think about a huge problem that is not meant for your age group, and kick its butt. If your older, and still want a shot to further develop your problem-solving skills, go ahead! Everyone should continue to do greatness in his or her lives. This is how they get there. Always take on a job for which you are under qualified. That is what challenges us to grow.

But, that's just me.

Logic In Middle Schools

I'm going to return here with a very simple question I would like you to ponder: How are students supposed to succeed in a course when they aren't even familiar with the building blocks?

The answer: They Can't!

Logic, as I mentioned before, was not even present in our curriculum until eighth grade, and even then the teachings of logic, both in the traditional sense and in regards to problem solving, were poorly done. As a result, a lot of students were dropping higher-level math courses, simply because they could not overcome the logic-disconnect they faced. These students, most of them with above-average intelligence, were failing because they were struggling with this new ideology and way of solving problems, because they didn't have the building blocks of logic to build off of. Yes, students dropping out could've been a result of hard material in general; however, when approximately 25% of students enrolled in advanced math classes drop out, you know something's up, more so than just involving the student's ability.

To give you a little more background as to what the class was actually like, I have summed up a decent part of the year in one sentence: The course we were supposed to be learning was Geometry, but ended up walking and talking like "Advanced Logic." For the first month or so, students were assigned incredibly, ridiculously, perplexingly complicated problems. The questions we were faced with were unlike anything we had ever seen. Most students, including myself, simply couldn't understand them. At the beginning of the year, in a faulty attempt at trying to counteract my lack of mathematical-logical ability, I attempted to try to suck up to the teacher to get some brownie points. It didn't work.

We were solving all types of equations, finding solutions to problems unlike anything we had seen before it, and everything else under the sun. A series of events that accurately described my own attempts at logic in class:

1.   The Problem was written down on the whiteboard, with 5 minutes allotted to try it on your own.

2.   30 seconds was allotted to copy down the problem (questions, diagrams, and everything else associated), in hopes that writing for as long as I could would make me seem smarter.

3.   3 minutes were used in an attempt to solve the problem during which multiple strategies at solving the task failed miserably.

4.   1 minute involved staring directly at the problem in hopes I would soon discover how to tell my brain to solve problems that I'd had never seen before and it would work.

5.   30 seconds were taken to act as if you were attempting the problem, but instead were doodling.

6.   The teacher answered the question with ease, as if it was as simple as single-digit multiplication, and you would move on to a new problem.

7.   Repeat steps 1-6 (with each next problem comes additional time to complete Step 6).

That about sums up my entire experience in the first month of 9th grade Geometry, as well as the experience of many around me (I could ascertain other students' failures as I was doodling).

Later in the year, after I had established myself as a fairly competent mathematician, I went up to my Geometry teacher and asked him, "Mr. Goldbeck, what was the whole deal with the beginning of the course?" To which he responded, "The foundations of logic, just to give you guys a little taste of how to solve problems you aren't used to." Obviously, I am paraphrasing, but wouldn't it have been great to learn a basis for logic in middle school?

As will soon be discussed, middle school math was a joke in regards to problem solving, so we should also incorporate practicing the skill of logic into our curriculum. I find it absurd that it is not. When I reflect upon Middle School, one of the things I recalled, and part of the motivation for this book, is that logic wasn't taught! No foundations, no hints that it might appear in the future. *Nada.*

In middle school, all students were exposed to the same experience. We were all given the most straightforward questions possible. No trouble, no difficulty. It was so basic that the entirety of the question bank either came from a packet, a worksheet, or another form of busywork that we had already completed in class. Although we were drilled frequently with practice sessions, we were rarely introduced to material that required thought.

Generally speaking, the mediocre-at-best questions we were assigned were taken directly from the class notes. It was as if we were being prepared for a fill in the blank test. You used exactly what you were taught, and nothing more. Most of the time, we just rearranged the numbers to fit the formulas or what we learned, and sometimes, the numbers even stayed the same!

At the risk of ranting, I repeat: Middle School provided no foundation of logic whatsoever. There was no natural progression from solving old problems and using them as a foundation to new, more complicated ones. After all, *that would be logical!*

Lastly, my personal pet peeve of middle school math is that there was no independent freedom to branch off. Students were asked not to do more or think outside the box in class, but rather, were expected to stick with the assigned and already trampled path towards boring-math success. Instead of encouraging students to expand their horizons, we were told to stick to the current material, and move at the pace of the teacher and class at large.

"Don't worry, we'll get to that later." "Don't worry, it'll be covered soon." "Trust me, you don't need to know that, because what I am teaching is the will of the almighty powers of Middle School Curriculum, and you shall stick to your assigned work and not worry about stuff that could potentially be important in the future because it will be covered sometime in the future and I don't care about it." All were some form of the common sound bites of my math teachers throughout the years, or at least my interpretation of them.

But the truth is that *later is too late!* There is no point learning something if you are only learning it because you need to get assigned material done. This, in fact, generates a lot of frustration with the entire aspect of logic in the middle school curriculum. The bottom line is that some students are more willing and more able than others, and teachers need to let those students explore their new and exciting logic-filled world. In matter of fact, many of these students ask to be given harder problems with more difficult work, because they felt they were lacking in actual math. Some students, such as myself, wanted to challenge each other and ourselves.

Now, logic utilization has so many incredible effects, especially in continually stretching one's mental capacity. This leads to an increase in overall critical thinking, thought leadership, and creative independence. Utilizing what one knows and turning it into something greater, that is the process of learning. Many may find the fact that kids are asking for more difficult work counterintuitive, but it's true. Learning is no longer simply a desire, but a necessity.

The main argument against teaching Logic is that it conflicts with current course material. But in all honesty, logic can easily be implemented into the curriculum.

One way it could be implemented is to tie it with courses at the beginning of each year. A repeated pattern of reviewing logic at the beginning of each year, followed up occasionally over the courses throughout middle school would've been so helpful. Even if only two weeks were devoted to logic every year, most students would still be able grasp the concept of using critical thinking to achieve success. In regards to anything involving a degree of difficulty, and with math in particular, the more accustomed one becomes to an aspect or to a unit, the clearer it becomes. Patterns are identified more quickly and problem solving comes more easily. Problems that were once unfamiliar can now be related to others. With practice, one can build up their abilities and apply logic to solve problems that may have seemed impossible before.

According to the article, "How to Teach Logic" by Martin Cothran, logic should begin to be taught to students around 12-13 years old, an age where our brains are like a sponge. Cothran says it's at this age that children want to uncover the truth to many happenings in their lives, as well as the peak time where students can begin to comprehend abstraction. In this article Cothran also points out:

"Children...have already encountered [abstract ideas] in mathematics. But, whereas mathematics deals with abstraction in the realm of quantitative relationships, logic deals with the abstraction in the realm of qualitative relationships. Both math and logic deal with abstraction, but math does it with quantities; logic (at least in its traditional form) does it with language."

I love this quote and believe it to be true. Cothran, like myself, believes middle school is the ideal time to start teaching kids about how to work with abstraction and think outside the box. A foundation in abstract thinking would begin at an age where currently there is nothing in place.

Now, again, some kids are unable to problem solve in a straightforward manner. Others believe that only some people have problem-solving skills, regardless of age. But I truly believe in the following maxim: Practice Makes Perfect (or close to it).

With anything you do in life, and as kids we're continually reminded of this, in that the more you practice - whether it be a sport or studying for a test - the more you get out of it. If this is valid, then why can't the same principle be applied to logic? Logic, in my opinion, should not be taught in a cookie-cutter style of definitions and formulas, but rather through practice and application of problem solving.

Expert Opinions

Deborah Meier

According to expert Deborah Meier, formal logic is incredibly important in many different aspects of life for middle school students. It's very similar to math itself, in that it has many applications in many fields of life.

Formal logic is the utilization of the fundamental habits of mind, she says. Logic involves the use of our brains to answer questions such as 'What if...' or 'How can you...' in order to reach a specific goal.

Logic, in Meier's mind, is the concept of being able to take apart ideas and to ask the fundamental questions that are necessary to complete tasks in life. Logic begs us to ask many questions pertaining to the situation at hand. This includes finding out what fundamental elements are present in certain circumstances; uncovering the interaction of each separate element in a problem; and, most importantly, how to use this information to go about getting an answer.

The basic concept of how to delve more deeply into any problem you have in life and break it down is extremely important, no matter what you are doing. These concepts can be applied to all disciplines. Science, Art, English; all of these subjects require the underlying logic that is demonstrated in Math. To look at things from different perspectives. To create new pathways. To ask thought provoking questions. To challenge the status quo. To think of change. To make change. All of these are the underlying principles of the ideologies of logic.

Meier also gave a great and relatable example. In art, when you are tasked with recreating a photograph by hand, you can use logic to succeed in your endeavor.

You can break it down first, by looking at and obtaining the essential elements that need to be included in your drawing. You then can see how these elements interact, with color, line, form, and all other Foundations and Principles of Art. Finally, you dive into recreating the image, using your pre-existing knowledge of drawing combined with the newfound information of the original drawing to successfully reconstruct your original picture, making it look as realistic as possible. I'm not an artist, yet I can still apply the basic principles of logic to succeed!

This brings up another important point: Logic can be applied to any and every situation, regardless of the degree of difficulty. From event planning, to solving word problems in math, to making changes to the food served in the school cafeteria; simply utilizing the fundamental habits of mind can result in success.

Meier believes the learning of logic is important not only because logic is utilized in such a prevalent way, but also because it is especially important that it be taught sooner rather than later. To summarize, it is imperative that logic is incorporated into middle school students, simply because middle school is the optimal time to succeed in mastering the incorporation of logic.

Finally, according to Meier, students in middle school need to learn the principles of formal logic. She believes these basic precepts are vital to the success of students. Meier elaborates on the fact that it is not acceptable for students to just learn the rules by memorization. How do rules work when you have to actually apply yourself to a question? I love to use Kevin Durant's quote from the movie "Thunderstruck" as an analogy for logic and learning. "Hard work beats talent when talent fails to work hard". In other words, Logic beats formulas when formulas fail to fit the problem.

Meier believes that teaching these principles to middle school students will encourage human intelligence to be utilized in a way that opens doors to all subject matter.

Andy Hunt

Andy Hunt, an expert in the field of computer programming, believes that, in regards to learning logic, "It depends what you mean by logic, but yes, at some level [students should learn logic]... Formal Boolean algebra? Maybe not, at least not at first, but many schools already start with set theory and such at pretty young ages."

Additionally, when commenting on other subjects he wished he had learned in middle school, Hunt talked about critical-thinking skills, something that I believe to be one and the same as logic.

He stated, "Critical thinking skills [are something I would've liked to see in middle school], in general. Programming depends on several inter-related skills, I think. This probably isn't a complete list, but let's start with:

1) Abstraction; being able to think in abstract terms (variables, higher-order concepts such as classes and objects,

data-streams, etc.). One of the keys aspects of programming is being able to "zoom in" and "zoom out" at 1000:1 ratio or more of different levels of abstraction.

2)   Logic (if-then-else, iteration, transfer of control, en-capsulation)

3)   Critical thinking; being able to analyze and reduce in-formation into a usable form, being able to judge the quality and source of information, that sort of thing.

None of these are really particular to writing software [with computer programming] itself, but I think are basic lit-eracy skills for the 21st century."

Regardless of the fact that logic in Hunt's life would mainly be used in programming, he has perfectly laid the outline for logic and critical thinking aught in schools.

Robert Goodman

Robert Goodman laid some important foundations for the importance of logic. In Goodman's mind, logic is the main function of school, from kindergarten throughout the rest of your life. As an example, he mentions how throughout your life, your ability to analyze situations and to create useful con-structs for life continues to develop and grow. Goodman even went as far as to say that all functions of the human race should be based on the need for logic!

Goodman more or less stated that logic equates to think-ing. Yes, you can call it critical thinking skills, but at the end of the day, logic comes down to intense thought. Goodman says that the facts, or "rules", of logic are unimportant, especially considering that through the use of technology, anyone can have immediate access to these rules; as such, they are unimportant to learn. However, logic can be learned and utilized in conjunction with the method demonstrated in the Math chapter, which I dubbed the "Round Table Method".

Logic requires problem solving, analytical thinking, and intense thought problem solving in spectacular ways. Goodman says that this does not specifically have to equate to math or science – rather, this can relate any subject, even to computer science. He even reflected about how he helped promote the AP Music class at his local High School; he believes that art and music can be utilized to learn logic and math at a similar level to subjects like math and science. In reality, Goodman remarks, any subject comes down to the utilization of analytical thinking. Goodman points out that the use of logic exists in all fields of human endeavor, and as such, the only difference from subject to subject is that *different domains have different applications*. So, at the end of the day, AP Music is as likely to develop logic as AP Calculus.

Paul Graham's Opinion

Paul Graham, the dual coder and entrepreneur, had a fresh perspective on logic.

When I asked him if he felt logic should be incorporated in middle schools, he responded with something unexpected. "It's amazing you asked that, because that is exactly what I'd been thinking. Conversations I've seen online have shown me what surprisingly large gaps many adults have in their understanding of logic. So many can't distinguish between necessary and sufficient conditions, for example. Society assumes people will just pick this stuff up along the way, but clearly they don't. So it seemed to me schools ought to teach it. At least tell everyone the names of the most common fallacies, so that when people committed them they could point their fingers and say 'begging the question.' Middle school seems the right time. This stuff is not as hard as the algebra a lot of kids get taught at that age."

And it is very true. Many adults around me are so unaware of the fact that the knowledge of logic is so important, and how it transfers to all walks of life; as such, we need to teach logic in middle schools, to ensure this gap in logical understanding doesn't become a cyclic pattern with our generation.

Conclusion

Logic plays an important role both in school as well as day-to-day, real world applications. The abilities of any one student to succeed in regards to facing any problem or situation are remarkable when that student is armed with logical thinking. Through the use of logic as well as with critical thinking skills, middle school students can further utilize their knowledge in such a way that they can succeed in anything, be it debate, sports, or just a friend-to-friend argument.

Therefore, I believe it is imperative that logic be further explained, taught, and stressed upon in middle schools.

CHAPTER 8

Public Speaking

P ublic Speaking – which I believe to be the way in which people orally present their ideas in a reasonable manner - is one of my greatest skills and assets. I utilize this style of effective communication almost daily in all areas of my life. To me, public speaking is so much more than it seems. It is the excitement that erupts when presenting your ideas in a captivating way, and the emotions for which you spread your ideas with. After all, effective public speaking, when done properly, is supposed to amplify anything and everything. Even the smallest accomplishment can be articulated as a major milestone. Now, with that said, shouldn't we need to provide middle school students with the capabilities to succeed in such an important circumstance such as this?

My Experience With Public Speaking

Take this book for example. I captivate my audience with vivid descriptions and immerse them in my verbiage, which is coupled with clear articulation. Then, when fortified with mounds of inflection, there is no one who is not entranced.

That was pretty good. Yes, this book might not be a great example of public speaking, considering it is written, but the same principles of good writing apply to public speaking. If this book was a speech, I really think it would kick ass.

Additionally, when I am at Debate Tournament, I have the confidence to go into each knowing I am going to do well. How could I not, when I couple my considerable public speaking experience with my ability to captivate the judges in a manner that is both astounding and winning? The scope of public speaking's importance, as well as its nuances, is the reason I wish public speaking were taught in Middle School.

Almost every student interviewed for this book agreed on one main ideology: Public Speaking is important and it should have be taught in middle school. It is arguably the most important skill anyone can have, and it is one of my top skills. The ability to orally communicate your ideas to any audience cannot be underestimated, in that effective public speaking will elevate anyone's ideas, profiles, abilities, and connections to new heights.

At this point, I assume most of us will agree that public speaking is an important skill. Those who don't can respectfully agree to disagree.

Having said that, here is the scariest fact of all: most young people have not developed this critical skill, and their public speaking skills, or lack of, do not cut it.

Unfortunately, many youths are unable to present themselves in an acceptable fashion. Now, yes, not everyone is going to be able to accomplish great public speaking, especially when nerves are a huge factor in regards to this. However, everyone can learn to conquer their nerves, or better still, to hide your nerves, are skills worth knowing, because they, along with public speaking, also translate to many other walks of life. You may not be able to rid yourself of your nerves; you just need to conceal them to appear relaxed and confident. This is something that can be done with practicing public speaking, at the prime time of middle school.

According to Graham Chapman, the business director at 919 Marketing (a PR and Marketing firm in North Carolina), "Too many recent grads are not equipped to present the company well over the phone or in person at networking events, new business meetings, etc. *If you can't speak [or] present yourself well, it is hard to help a company drive business.*"

This is a problem, plain and simple. Lack of teaching for this important 21st century skill is resulting in an absence of critical skills necessary to excel in the real world - the business world. Kids should not have to enter the real world at a disadvantage, especially one that pertains to a skill so essential yet simple in its nature. I simply cannot imagine why it is not being taught. Which begs the question, why isn't public speaking being taught in middle school?

Public Speaking in Middle Schools

To be blatantly honest, there was virtually no real, useful, or informative introduction to Public Speaking in middle school. Perhaps I shouldn't say that. Once in 6th grade, we did a project in which we had a 2-minute oral exam. All it amounted to, however, was ill prepared kids sputtering words in front of the class, and checkmarks were assigned for "Speaking Ability – PASS". You also know that there is a huge problem when the kid with a pallet expander – yes that would be me - gets a 9 out of 10 for clarity. Anyone who has ever had a 'mouth full of marbles' - otherwise known as wearing a pallet expander, retainer, or whatever other orthodontic contraption was in your mouth - can certainly appreciate that it's hard to get out three syllables properly, let alone give a full presentation and deserve to receive a good grade on it.

Bad Public Speaking

The results of inadequate public speaking skills are many and varied. The following are just a few examples: Filler Words while speaking, Inability to speak (spontaneously), and lack of confidence and comfort when presenting.

Let's first discuss filler words. "Like" is a prime example of a Filler Word – they are just stupid words that are used to connect sentences in an oral presentation – and to elaborate further, I'll tell a little story. I love stories, don't you? One of my classmates over the years has always had a problem overusing the word 'like'. When we first met, and still to this day, I did not honestly think he or she possessed the capability to go three complete sentences without sputtering out the dreaded 'like'. Because of this, sometimes things they had to say, which were informative and intelligent, often sounded like jumbled garbage. Bottom Line: Excessive use of this term led to occasional teasing at the hands of other classmates.

So, the implication here is that more than just their communication skills were compromised. I understand that filler-words are words that we use to transition, fill in the blanks, and use between the points we are trying to make; I use them sometimes to. But, sometimes, they aren't even words! Think: 'um', 'like', 'kinda', 'sorta' – almost everybody uses them, yet nobody likes them. While useful in certain situations and in a limited capacity - such as the need to stall for time when you have forgotten the next word in your presentation - an effort needs to be made to keep them to a minimum. Overuse of these "fillers" dramatically reduces the impact of your words on others. Imagine trying to have an intelligent conversation with someone and every third word in the chat is 'like' or 'um'. This is a disadvantage that kids simply do not need; we have enough to deal with already. Try getting an adult to take you seriously. That in itself can be a monumental task. Trust me on that! Additionally, as excerpted from a great article from http://sixminutes.dlugan.com/stop-um-uh-filler-words/, excellent points were made about Filler Words:

"They contribute nothing, and weaken your effectiveness as as a speaker in two primary ways:

Filler words represent verbal static that has to be filtered out by your audience. (It's one of the communication barriers cited in a recent article by guest author Stacey Hanke.) Why say it if the audience has to immediately filter it out?

Repeated and excessive use of filler words weakens your credibility. It may be perceived as indicating lack of preparation, lack of knowledge, or lack of passion. All of these perceptions are bad for you."

This was an incredible piece, and for more on filler words, check out the full article. This is just one example of something necessary that can be practiced and fixed in middle school.

Next, let's talk about the inability of students to speak off-the-cuff. While writing this book in 9th and 10th grade, which I've mentioned earlier, I was a member of the speech and debate club at my high school. My event was "Extemporaneous Speaking," meaning I was given a question about recent current events varying from economics to politics, then given 30 minutes to prepare a 7 minute speech, which would be presented to a judge. For some people that might seem like a Herculean task. It might seem impossible! But it's really not.

A skilled "Extemper," or really just anyone who practices for several days, can develop the ability to speak for seven minutes. We learned and practiced how engaging content combined with humor equals great public speaking, and how to go about doing it. However, when I joined the club, I was stunned by the number of kids who were inept at speaking off the cuff. A prime example of this is that I could have a conversation with someone ten minutes prior to their speech, at which time they were able to convey information with precise detail and strong content, where their tone of voice and pitch was excellent. It was evident that they had the skills and tools to present a well-delivered speech. Unfortunately, however, during their speech, that practice they had given me became unrecognizable. They would mumble for the majority of their presentation, they wouldn't make eye contact and they could not be heard – even from across a classroom. Although they knew how to deliver a great speech, nerves and lack of practice meant that they were unable to present the speech in a more casual, conversational style to the judge. The delivery was more consistent with a presentation than a public demonstration of speaking "off the cuff". If the topic had been unfamiliar, then by all means, it's not their fault. But if it was something that had been spoken about with perfect clarity only 10 minutes prior, with understanding and knowledge, then you know that these kids are having trouble with public speaking.

In the event, and I'm trying to say this without meaning to sound the least bit cocky: I was simultaneously incredibly good while being incredibly bad. Once I got the idea of what I was about and what I wanted to say, I developed the ability to use 5 out of the 30 minutes to prepare, and then spend the other 25 minutes relaxing, talking to my friends, making new ones, and much more. I was even able to take a nap once before a speech! And I was pretty good at it. With minimum effort and very little practice, I managed to defeat every other 9th grader at the Statewide Competition in my event and placed 7th place out of all 9th graders and 10th graders. I defeated kids who had practiced and practiced for long stretches of times, some even attending summer camps for the event, by employing some simple charm and the use of some basic concepts.

It's possible that I was simply better than the kids - but when I had the chance to listen to my contemporaries and opponents, I found that it wasn't that I was so spectacular, but rather that many of them were terrible; it was not so much that I won, but that they lost. Many were mumbling, others failed to master any eye contact; I think you get the picture. Even with effort and hard work, kids today struggle with speaking spontaneously.

The ability to speak spontaneously and conversationally is an important life skill. Why? If, for example, you are a teenager seeking employment and you happen to run into your potential boss, who interviewed you the day before, you would like to have an intelligent conversation. What if he approached you and asked a few follow-up questions? Wouldn't you like to sound mature and well spoken? I know I would!

Adults: what if you wanted to get a drink with your friends, you don't want to be judged on your conversation skills and found lacking.

And, last but not least, Middle School and High School students: What if you were taking a 'verbal test' which required short answers but you don't have any idea of where or how to begin to answer the question correctly and efficiently? It is so important that kids be given the opportunity to develop excellent speaking skills. If they do not, then they may be losing opportunities due to the inability to communicate with people who are more educated. If one's potential is judged and found lacking based on communication skills, opportunities may immediately vanish into thin air. Again, lack of ability for speaking off the cuff is just another example of the negative results of not incorporating public speaking into the curriculum.

I believe that the best way to incorporate public speaking into the curriculum would be by having many 'practice tests', and training students to be great public speakers through much practice. I believe that this is the only way to learn how to speak, by continuing to practice and get better by learning *yourself* through *your own speeches*. Obviously, the person listening to your speeches is going to be extremely helpful; I am forever grateful for my 9th grade Forensics captain Peter, who taught me the ways in which to excel at public speaking. All in all, the whole way to practice public speaking and get better is through small practice sections, be it with fellow students, one-on-one with the teacher, or in front of the entire class itself. This does not matter much, as all that counts is the ability to learn through your practice speeches.

Expert Opinions

Bill Ayers

Bill Ayers strongly believes that public speaking is a critical skill, and supports my belief that it should be taught in middle school. He elaborates how public speaking is absolutely critical that one have the ability to stand up and have a voice in a public forum. People need to stand up for themselves and succeed as it pertains to oral persuasion. And there is no better time to establish this than in Middle School.

Ayers cites his favorite example of public speaking as a Chicago Poetry Slam. A little unconventional, yes, but it is his opinion that learning to speak in front of an audience is essential in the lives of young people, and this is an example like all others. It builds confidence, and forces you to projects confidence. It builds people up in the eyes of others. It is something so different; you either fear and loathe it or love and cherish public speaking.

Without a doubt, practice makes perfect, and this is particularly true of public speaking! In Ayers' opinion, the middle school years are a critical time of development. Great success in public speaking, the ability to be fluid and relaxed whether speaking or responding to questions, is directly related to beginning the journey at a young age: 11, 12, and 13.

Finally, Ayers mentions the fact that public speaking is an example of a basic act of liberty. The ability to speak, the ability to write, and the ability to read are all liberties provided to Americans. This is why public speaking is so important; in order to act on your liberties, and to do it well, you need to practice skills that will maximize your voice, both literally and figuratively speaking. Improving your public speaking skills is an excellent way to achieve this. All in all, Ayers gave some interesting, unconventional thought in regards to public speaking, but correct ones nonetheless.

Terri Sjodin

Terri Sjodin is a highly respected speaker and author, and has inspired and trained thousands to become better public speakers themselves. She has graciously agreed to share her expertise on How to become an Awesome Public Speaker.

One of the most critical things to learn in public speaking is how to captivate the audience with your voice, she says.

This includes learning how to project your voice, so that everyone can hear you, you can manage the pitch and tone of your voice (so that it is pleasant to the ear), and you can be aware of your facial expressions and body language. All contribute to the effective communication of your message; in fact, only about 7% of your message is conveyed by the words alone!

These skills are essential to deliver a great oral performance and are developed by those who go into 'improv', standup comedy, poetry slams, and live theatre. The successful orator is concerned not only with what is said, but HOW it is said. Middle school students can be taught these skills, and Terri expressed that she is a big supporter of learning public speaking at this age.

Sjodin was able to take advantage of certain opportunities at a young age because of her speaking abilities, and said it breaks her heart that others would not be offered the same chance because of a lack of confidence and ability in the realm of public speaking.

These opportunities sparked her interest in public speaking, and prompted her to join the speech and debate team in high school, where she further developed the skills she uses today. So she has become a big proponent of developing verbal communication skills, because it is one of the most powerful skillsets to have. It breaks down barriers and builds bridges between communities and people. It connects thought leaders to their audience, so that they're able to share ideas and thought leadership.

In Sjodin's mind, the best public speakers are able to create a conversation while on the stage; if you can deliver a clear, concise message, it becomes the *ultimate equalizer*. In those moments, it doesn't matter where you came from or what separates you from another. When you speak beautifully, and from the heart, it levels the playing field between people from different backgrounds and promotes equal opportunity while fostering collaboration.

Additionally, Sjodin says it is a great misnomer that we must only prepare for public speaking to large audiences. She said that it's actually more important to be comfortable speaking in front of small groups. This is because in day-to-day life, you're more likely to have to present in front of your co-workers in business meetings. If you want a great job, you'll need to be well spoken in the interview and beyond. If your dream is to do a speaking engagement in front of media, you still need to engage the audience. The skills required are the same regardless of the format.

In order to do this well, you must be successful at speaking and presenting under pressure. Practice is essential, not optional. Sjodin recommends speaking at any kind of public forum to gain some experience. There is no substitute for experience. In the words of Nike: Just Do It!

When asked how this could be implemented in Middle Schools, Sjodin recalled her experience with show and tell as a child. She said that we should definitely re-introduce it, because it's not as daunting as "public speaking". And yet that is exactly what it is. However, it's meant to be fun and informal and it gets kids comfortable with the idea of speaking a group of people. Story telling is an art that is refined through repetition. Nothing more and nothing less.

Sjodin says that practicing for class presentations is another great way to become comfortable with public speaking. She recalled her first experience: she was in the 5th grade, and she entered her first speech competition. It was for 5-8th graders from different schools and it was sponsored by the high school to encourage more kids to learn about public speaking. The event was created to generate interest in the speech and debate team in high school. Participants might potentially seek out more opportunities for public speaking. Sjodin said this was a great introduction to public speaking, and it captured her interest and engaged her in a way that inspired her to pursue it as a career in later life.

Conclusion

Public speaking is kind of like cleaning your room; at the beginning, it may be terrible, you may hate it, you may be *bad* at it, but at the end of the day, you're going to appreciate having the clean room, and now can clean rooms for the rest of your life.

That was a weird analogy, but it does work (to some degree). The bottom line is that Public Speaking is an essential 21st century skill, one that should be incorporated into middle school curriculums.

CHAPTER 9

Computer Programming

I magine a career opportunity that is almost too good to be true. One field that, by 2020, will have approximately 400,000 people working in the field, but there will be about 1,400,000 total job opportunities at that same time period. Yep. That's a million more jobs than people in only that one field. A potential $500 BILLION field, according to current estimations. A market untouched, untapped, primed for growth. Yet for some reason, it's not taught in middle schools. This is yet another subject that Middle School didn't teach students, putting them at a disadvantage in regards to helping them pursue incredible future endeavors and open new opportunities for them.

Now, what's the field you might ask? It's the one, the only.... COMPUTER PROGRAMMING!

In my opinion, computer programming should be the absolute first priority to the education of students everywhere, considering its vast possibilities, limitless job market in the future, as well as the fact that, in my opinion, it's the coolest thing ever.

Coding in Middle School

I'll tell you what I was taught pertaining to Computer Programming in Middle School - nothing. Middle school computer science was an utter failure and waste of time in the eyes of my peers and I.

Story Time. In 7th grade, every student in my school had to take a mandatory 'elective' called technology. It was considered a joke of a class, where you didn't do much but sit around and maybe watch the movie 'October Sky' a few times.

However, during the middle of that school year, we actually started to do *something*: we were dabbling in computer programming. Specifically, website creation.

Naturally, I was excited to begin this incredible new endeavor, one that could potentially be thrilling and eye opening. And naturally, I was let down.

Instead of learning new and exciting skills, or participating in constructive activities designed to motivate us to pursue computer science further, my monotonously-toned teacher, dubbed 'The Kernel', just droned on and on about the programming language of HTML (HyperText Markup Language). This is the language that creates any website, specifically setting up how content on a website is displayed. To give you an idea, with this language, you can tell the computer to display one line as a big header, and set another line as a bulleted list, among hundreds of other 'tags'. This is also known as the boring part of computer programming.

Now, rather than allowing us students to explore coding and to delve into exciting new possibilities, as would be given with almost everything else BUT HTML, we were given uneventful, step-by-step instructions of what to type in, and we followed the teacher blindly.

We would get into class, sit down on our computers, and 'The Kernel' would proceed to give us the necessary instructions to type into the computers, verbatim. The following dialogue accurately describes the entirety of a typical class:

(Bell Rings)

"The Kernel': Ok guys, turn on your computers.

Students: (Grunts)

"The Kernel': Open up Notepad (a very simple and small application on your desktop allowing you to input code).

Students: (Grunts)

"The Kernel': Type in this – '<html>' (goes through 15 more lines of code spoon-fed to us)

"The Kernel': Does anyone not get it?

Students: (Grunts)

Now, this might be considered *fundamentally successful* in teaching students, but in practicality, it really missed the mark.

As an intermediate-level programmer in the field of computer science, *who learned how to code in all the wrong ways*, I can tell you that this type of learning environment is not one destined for success in computer programming.

First off, you can't learn through typing verbatim someone else's premade code. Rather than teaching us something substantial, The Kernel only taught us how to copy blindly, similar to copying down a PowerPoint slide but not understanding anything on it.

This is not the way to teach computer science. Computer science is supposed to be something students can use to explore possibilities, while possessing the backbones of a solid foundation. Students should learn through a variety of other methods, which we will discuss more in depth later on. Are you supposed to learn about a foreign language by just copying down notes from a whiteboard? So, in the end of the day, what I was learning deterred me from wanting to continue in a field that is now my passion.

While on the subject, it should be noted that I feel 'front-end' website creation, or what the viewer can see, is not what students should be learning as a first language in today's world as it pertains to computer programming. As found through my own personal endeavors and research, the best approach for an absolute beginner is to dabble in the basics of the Python programming language, which I'll get more into later on. Overall, it's important to know that there are so many different languages and pathways to go into and follow for programming mastery; web development is just the wrong path for a first timer to make. This is mostly because of the advent of drag and drop website creators, like Squarespace, which make front-end design unimportant for the most part. However, I still think it is a good thing to know down the line, just not as a first language.

This aside, many kids don't even have the opportunity to learn how to computer program in middle school! Most middle schools do not place high enough importance on this skill, which is arguably one of the most important fields in today's world.

Now, computer programming is extremely important to the lives of students, and not just because of the fact that it could potentially make them rich in the future.

Firstly, learning to code can help you in a bunch of other classes, as well as in life generally.

For instance, many students are going to pursue a future that will involve the construction of a website. Whether it is an eager student making a personal site, such as is the case with me (AaronLafazan.com), or it is an entrepreneur hungry to put his company on the web, or even someone with a passion and wants to write about their ideas on a blog, they need a platform to "host" their writing.

All of these scenarios involve the creation of websites, and by learning website creation in middle school, students could potentially save a lot of money. Instead of outsourcing the project to some lucky person who was able to learn how to code, where many spend up to $4,000 to receive a well-done website, students in the future could create their own platforms, or even charge other adults to make websites.

This is just one prime *real life example* of how coding can affect almost anybody; coding is all around us, whether we choose to admit it or not.

What Needs To Be Taught

There are many paths in which computer programming can be taught, each with their own individual strengths and weaknesses.

Personally, I've found that the best path for a newcomer to computer programing I have found is to start with a language called Python. Python is a programming language that has many components that make it an incredible programming language for beginners, more so for easy understanding than anything else.

To start off, Python is a very friendly and easy to learn language. When learning to program, one thing that can overwhelm you is the complexity of many lines of code, and Python can help ease that anxiety. The first task or two that almost every tutorial on a programming language will show you is how to write the phrase "Hello World!" to the screen. This is common, and for the most part, it's a simple and harmless thing to write. However, many languages make this normally easy task seem like something taken out of a horror film.

With a language like C++, you end up with something monstrous just for one line. It looks like this on the following pate (the arrow is meant to demonstrate the line number):

C++ Hello World

```
>#include <iostream>

>using namespace std;


>int main()

{

    cout <<  "Hello World"
    system( "PAUSE" );
    return 0;


}
```

Now, in Python, to print out Hello World on the console, you simply type the following phrase:

Python Hello World

```
> print "Hello World"
```

Done, plain and simple, right?

I hope you catch my drift. Python is a language that offers the simplicity a beginning coder desires, especially because Python is *syntactically* very close to English. It's so easy and clean; I love it!

As another example to demonstrate Python's simplicity, let's go over some words used to make a function. The keyword 'def' is used to 'define' a function (a program that takes an input, runs the code inside the program, and generates an output); the keyword 'print' is used to 'print' anything to the main console; and the keyword 'var' signals that a 'variable' is going to be created. Simple, logical and user-friendly.

<u>Sample Python Function</u>

```
>def DoSomething():

    >value = 1
    >return value
```

Another great example of why it's great for beginners is the way the language was created. Each language on Earth, such as with English, Spanish, and Mandarin, has its very own syntax (its own rules of sentence structure and vocabulary). Similarly, each computer programming language has its own requirements for certain terms to be typed out to produce your end goal.

Now, what makes python so special is its incredibly simple and beginner-friendly syntax. For instance, you write code in Python with a method called 'tabbing'. As you can see in the diagram of a python function above, when you need to run a specific program to accomplish a task, you use 'indentation,' so the computer can understand your program. Under the line where you declare your program's name, you then indent the next line, to show your computer that that next line is involved with whatever was stated above. In addition, as you saw with the 'Print' function, it certainly does not take a whole lot to produce something. This type of clean and simple syntax is awesome, because it teaches the beginner how to write 'clean code.'

Another real-life analogy comes to when you are taking notes; don't you want to be able to look back at them later and understand what you were learning in class? As such, you don't want your notes all over the place; rather, you want them to be organized with a good flow. With clean functions like the ones that result from writing code in Python, you can easily interpret what you have written and know what the program does, the method the coder went about programming that program, etc. Also, the necessity for indentation leads programmers down the line to have good indentation, even when programming in languages that don't require any indentation at all.

All in all, Python is an incredible language, one that is very simple to read and easy to implement and learn; I'd definitely recommend it as a first time language.

Another very common language that is incredible for young, ambitious beginner programmers who are believed to not have the skills required to write actual code is called Scratch.

According to the main page FAQ on scratch.org, "Scratch is a programming language and online community where you can create your own interactive stories, games, and animations - and share your creations with others around the world. In the process of designing and programming Scratch projects, young people learn to think creatively, reason systematically, and work collaboratively."

In short, it's a stroke of brilliance for young kids who are coding for the first time. It works by putting together several different literal 'blocks' of code in order to create one chain-reaction type effect. In lieu of writing code, you connect literal blocks that possess commands you want to execute, in order to ensure the code is as user-friendly as possible before the code execution.

As an example, instead of writing the code for a picture of a dolphin to move across the screen, you drag and drop the appropriate block, which has its specific instructions, on the appropriate spot. Each block has many interchangeable parts, such as the speed at which the dolphin would move across the screen, as well as the direction the dolphin would travel before reaching its destination.

Now, I could probably take up the entirety of this book with different programming languages to teach, and different paths to take, but I'm not going to. Python and Scratch are just the best representations of first-time languages.

How We Should Teach Computer Programming

Another important question to consider in any case of implementing something new in a curriculum is "*How* should students learn computer programming?"

Now, there are a variety of different answers with different techniques. Keep in mind, there's no right answer, just different styles with different results, similar to the different programming languages.

As an example, I'll show Thomas Cormen's approach, a computer science professor at Dartmouth (who you'll hear more from later), which entails a method that is very well thought out, and one that I feel would greatly help middle school students.

During class with the students, Cormen would focus on having students understand what the pieces of the larger puzzle are. For instance, in class one, he would teach the main difference between Linear Searching and Binary Searching, two separate types of algorithms that have really fancy names, both of which can be used to search a list of practically infinite length. It would just be regular, short, informative class lectures.

He then would give students very short assignments, which would be due the next class. These would not be intended to take a long time, but rather, they would serve as a refresher of the learned material through practice; it's like a better version of regular homework. He would continue assigning these assignments until he felt that enough knowledge had been assimilated on that specific topic.

The next step would be to give out a Lab assignment. These, he said, would entail a substantial amount of important, informative, and helpful array of assignments, with students getting a week to complete this comprehensive assignment. With this lab assignment, students would have to put together the little things they had learned, with their smaller homework practices and class lectures, in order to make something interesting.

In summary, he would start with simple homework assignments to ensure students are kept on track, which would complement the in-class lectures, and then he would give students something more substantial to grow their skills, the labs, which would complete the student's knowledge by forcing him to learn through his experience creating programs and such. His analogy of the process is that his simple homework showed "How you hammer a nail", while the lab assignments would show "How you make a birdhouse," forcing the student to put together all of his knowledge to make something cool and exciting.

Cormen has found this method to be very successful, mainly because the only way to learn programming is to *actually do it*. Not to read books, not to watch someone program, but to get your hands dirty and write the code yourself. As such, his method provides the opportunity for success across the board no matter what you are trying to accomplish.

There are so many more methods of learning programming, many of which are written later on, but Cormen's formula is a prime example in which one should teach computer programming

Computer Programming in Middle Schools

Now, the same question arises: why should computer programming be taught in middle school?

It's not because of an early learning advantage. If you start learning how to computer program at any age your fine. Learning how to code in High School? You're golden! Learning how to code in College? Fine, you're well off! Learning how to code as a middle aged man who got laid off and needs to find a new career? Go for it, your good to go!

No matter what age you start learning to code, you are totally fine, and have a head start on many others. But, starting to learn to code at middle school is absolutely, unequivocally the best opportunity you can provide today's students with.

Most kids, if they start to learn through school, begin in high school, starting anywhere between 14 to 18 years old. This means that these students, at most, can graduate high school possessing a maximum of 1 - 4 years of experience in computer coding. Now this is certainly fantastic, and is an excellent head start, putting students on the right path with programming.

But, what if kids could start to learn computer programming in middle school? The ages of kids in middle school range from 11 to 14. So now, these students can come out of elementary school, start to learn how to code at a young age, and then come out of high school with anywhere from 4 - 7 years of coding experience! How incredible is that? Imagine all students coming out of school with seven years of experience in any field! The possibilities are endless.

Current Developments With Programming

On September 16th 2015, New York City Mayor Bill de Blasio mandated that within 10 years, all of the public high schools under the domain of New York City would be required to offer computer science courses to all students.

This act will ensure that all students under these schooling zones have at least some basic exposure to computer science. This is where it gets more abstract, as this can imply a plethora of different pathways, entailing everything from the building of robots to learning to use very simplistic and basic programming languages, like the Scratch language (mentioned above).

However, in the end of the day, I feel that this legislation, and similar pieces of legislation, such as laws set up in San Francisco to accomplish similar results in computer science, help take a step forward in the right direction with tackling the problem of the lack of computer science education. If we could get all students on the right track, and put them on the path of computer programming, than an incredible amount of interests could be sparked and countless brains could be fed with computer science knowledge.

Overall, I feel that this could potentially be one of the greatest pieces of legislation ever enacted. My only regret with the legislation is that I believe it should have been extended into all middle schools as well.

Expert Opinions

Thomas Cormen

According to Thomas H. Cormen, co-author of *Introduction to Algorithms*, Dartmouth Professor, and one of the most knowledgeable men on the subject of Computer Science, all students are going to need to learn how to code on some level.

As we move farther into the 21st Century, knowledge of how to program is going to be essential in order to complete tasks using the computer. Cormen talked about how people are going to be using computers in the future, and there is a very high likelihood you are probably going to end up having to do something involving computer programming.

Now, whether this entails creating rules for a formula in regards to how to block spam out of your email account, or performing several scripts on a Microsoft Excel spreadsheet to manipulate data and text information, most people are going to have to be involved in some task that is strongly related to programming with computers.

Computer programming isn't even a skill as much as it is a form of literacy, he says. In the future, it's not going to be enough if you simply know how to use a computer at a basic level. Here, many confuse the concepts of thinking that they 'know about computers.' These are differentiated, as one who is technically skilled possesses the ability to complete real actions on a computer, like coding programs to *make* video games, while non-technical people know how to *play* video games. It is very important in that regard that people need to understand how to use computers, and to know how to properly manipulate their machines to complete certain tasks.

Now, in regards to programing as a whole, some are going to be successful in this endeavor; but there are going to be many other students who it's not going to work for. Some students either don't like it, or aren't ready for it at the point in time where they tried to learn it. Moral of the story: computer programming, especially at the middle school age, isn't for everyone.

Cormen even went on to tell me a story as to how at one point in his teaching career at Dartmouth, he thought he could teach anyone the ways of computer science and how to program well. He soon realized, however, that he simply couldn't teach these skills to everyone. There are going to be several kids who aren't going to get it. It's like how some kids won't understand an aspect of math, or someone won't be able to write certain genres in English. Many kids won't resonate with what they are being taught, but overall, he believes that it is an absolute wonderful thing for students to experiment with.

Cormen and I also discussed the turn-offs that are associated in computer coding. Many are hesitant to learn to code, for example, because many believe that a lot of people think that you have to be a math whiz in order to be a computer programmer.

This is a common myth Cormen shared with me, which I've heard of before. Many think computer coding is very math heavy, and because many people aren't good at math or they don't like math, they believe they cannot succeed in coding. This is not true though; only in the very upper echelons of coding is math necessary to excel.

Additionally, many are scared of the fact that you might 'screw up your computer'. Cormen said a large number of people are afraid of what is going to happen to their computer when they run programs. They think that they might 'break' the computer. So, what's the absolute worst thing that can happen? You screw up a few things? You could always just go out and buy a new computer, and learn from your mistakes. So, for those of you that have these fears, you can trust the Professor, and know there are no problems that should interfere in you learning to computer code.

Guido Van Rossum

Another great expert on the topic of coding is the man, the myth, the legend, known as the 'Benevolent Dictator of Life' by the coding community, is Guido van Rossum. Van Rossum is arguably the most important coder of our generation. He has created something so revolutionary, it changes coding today: the Python programming language, which we have already talked about extensively.

When asked about his thoughts on young kids learning to code, Van Rossum gave an interesting perspective. He talked about how computer programming is such a specialized skill that most students learning hardly scratch the surface of programming in their introductory classes. For this reason, and the constant complexities and changes in coding, he is very hesitant to have kids pick up computer programming skills at such a young age, since the language they learn most likely won't even be relevant by graduation.

However, he fully encourages having some understanding of the 'magic' of computers, based off of the exploration of hardware and software. All in all, he believes that it's more important to understand what goes on, and to have a clear view of everything in totality, rather than just hone in on one aspect.

Van Rossum feels the best approach to teach kids how to code is to teach different languages at different ages. This is because the ability for abstract thinking develops over time, and thus increases your programming abilities. He recommended that kids should start with something very concrete, like Scratch. Van Rossum mentioned that the Scratch system is one that was carefully designed to be easy, accessible, and is able to run on every computer, which is especially helpful to kids in poorer neighborhoods who want to pursue programming.

Now, Scratch is not used in professional programing, so students can focus on exploring interest in those areas, as opposed to memorizing syntax (which is so incredibly boring, trust me). You can learn what types of things computers can do without worrying about the 'bureaucratic details' of how it works and how to do it. This, he says, will give students the chance to have fun with programming.

After a while though, the Scratch system will become less interesting, and other systems become more so. Opportunities like another MIT system, which focuses on Android App Development, App Inventor, is another great system to take advantage of. These different opportunities open up different parts of the world, and allow for different ways of communication with programming, he says.

He said that when students are at the point where they begin to learn formal computer science, possibly in their last year of Middle school, then they could begin to learn something like Python. Van Rossum said this language is used even in the professional world, loved by companies like Google, and for this reason, he wouldn't start young middle school students with Python. He says that it has far too many complexities to be taught at the younger portion of middle school.

Another thing that Van Rossum said needed to be taught was the concept of Algorithms. Now, there are a huge variety of different Algorithms and Data Structures (which sound much more intimidating than they actually are), but many of these realistically aren't worth teaching until college, or even post-college. Van Rossum talked about how students at the middle school ages should focus on the "fun" algorithms, as opposed to the math-heavy, extremely complicated ones.

Just to name a couple, these 'fun algorithms' include approximating the value of Pi and calculating prime numbers. He also says, in his professional experience, the majority of code that's written is not made up on these types of algorithms, so it's fine for kids to explore with them.

Van Rossum also heavily discussed about was simple logic. Simple logic is extremely important throughout coding, he says, especially with understanding programming concepts, such as 'if statements' and 'loops'. Simple logic is also important for a large part of code in itself; thinking about implementing a game, the fundamental algorithms for implementing the physics of a game, and configuring the 3rd Dimension in your program are all types of tasks that need to be conquered through the use of simple logic in the functions of programming.

When asked what is the best way to teach kids, Van Rossum admitted that for him personally, he was a special case in regards to learning to program. When he had first learned to code, there wasn't much information out there, nor were there many programs to fool around with like the ones we have today. When he first got into it, however, he was very good at it, unaffected by the lack of resources. And overall, because of his natural ability to pick it up, he had a hard time teaching programming, he remarked, especially to those who didn't have lots of prior experience already.

However, Van Rossum did share how he had met many educators' who had lots of experience teaching general computer science in recent time. He said that the interesting thing was with meeting these educators is that if you talk to four different educators, you're going to end up with five different opinions on how kids should learn to program, demonstrating how there is no one designated path.

All in all, Van Rossum believes that a good path, one that can accomplish what is necessary to move on from beginner status, is to start with Scratch, then focus on HTML (the language powering the display of the content you see on the web), and then Python.

However, much of coding, something that any programmer can attest to, is about finding the problem in your code. You must be able to find the answer to, 'Why does it not do what I want?' It is very educational to find the bug in which you find the problem yourself, and so Van Rossum mentioned that is best to give students a project, something reasonable to build, and to learn along the way to *debug* the problems themselves.

Bjarne Stroustrup

Bjarne Stroustrup, the creator of the C++ programming languages and one of the greatest minds we have in programming, was very helpful in formulating an idea of middle school coding.

When asked his thoughts on young kids learning to code, Stroustrup gave a very interesting answer, "I think it's easy to start children on 'coding' too early. I suggest that 'coding' for young people (pre-high-school or even pre-university) should be in the context of projects that are not just code. Robots, data analysis for biology, and physics experiments could be good examples. Cheap computers (e.g., Raspberry Pie) for control of physical 'gadgets' could be important. Simply teaching programming as an academic skill (like Math or Physics) is unlikely to scale for lack of interest and lack of sufficiently good teachers.

There are so many topics that it would be good for young people to study that early coding isn't high on my priority list: such as, history, literature, mathematics, physics, natural languages, and biology. All could and should be taught in greater depth and with greater intensity than is common in US schools. We have lots of evidence that people can become superb programmers and great scientists without having seen a line of code before they were 20. We should educate people, not merely train them for a specific task or career."

He also regarded that, "Before high school, I think young people should be taught programming only where some coding skills are needed for some other task."

Even though we may disagree in a small sense, I do agree that it would be optimal if we would teach students code in an overall sense of things, teaching 'in context', as opposed to flat out teaching computer programming for the sake of knowing it at a young age.

Additionally, when asked how he felt students should be taught, he responded, "Through projects that are not just putting together poor websites. The purpose must be to help people to think in a logical manner and use tools to achieve goals. Teaching programming in isolation from other topics would just impoverish an education. Programming must be part of a balanced education. People who know only programming and a few related technical skills can become very narrow and miserable people."

Overall, Stroustrup, a brilliant man who provided profound solutions in his excellent overview of a new style of teaching code, in a general, combination type of coding.

Paul Graham

Programmer, entrepreneur, and brilliant mind Paul Graham also added very interesting thought to middle school computer programming.

When asked about his perspective on young kids learning to program, Graham responded, "I think all kids should learn how to program at some point. I'm not sure what the right age is. And of course before they write programs, they can do various forms of proto-programming, like combining functional blocks. There's almost no lower age limit for that if you make it simple enough."

This could potentially equate to the learning of Scratch programing, or something similar, or simply watching a teacher demonstrate programs. This was a view that aligned with the rest of the chapter.

He coupled this with the information kids should be learning with computer science: "It's pretty obvious what will be most engaging: programs that manipulate something you can see. Then the set of things you can manipulate grows with time. When Seymour Papert started working on Logo, all you could do was draw simple pictures, and that took expensive hardware. Now you can manipulate 3D models, or control a robot. In the future it will be possible to do even more interesting things."

Graham is really saying that the *what* itself does not necessarily matter, as long as you make the subject of the programming manipulation one such that the results can be exciting and captivating.

He provides an interesting perspective on the young programming world, which he further goes on to share why many are hesitant to learn to code: "I think it's the same thing that makes people afraid of math. Formal reasoning is hard for a lot of people. It is uncomfortably constraining.

Plus the way they're taught compounds their dislike. Hard ideas are sort of like healthy food. If you cook healthy ingredients cleverly, they can be delicious. But if you're a clumsy cook, and also believe healthy food has to taste bad to be good for you, then you're going to produce some pretty awful meals."

Overall, Graham gave incredible insight into the overall nature of programming and the interactions of young middle school students and computer science, and is very on point as to the rest of this chapter in totality.

Andy Hunt

Andy Hunt also had a lot to say on the topic of teaching programming. Hunt, an experienced programmer and author on computer science, wrote that, "I think it [learning to code] is an absolute necessity for any country that wants to remain globally competitive. A basic understanding of programming is the new literacy; folks who do not understand computers and information science will find it increasingly harder to get a job. Any job, anywhere. In the old days, you didn't always have to be smart to get a job; there were plenty of low-skill and semi-skilled jobs available. Many of these jobs are already gone, and in the not-too-distant future, they'll all be gone. Robots and factory automation will be the norm. We already have whole factories in China with no humans; it's all automatic."

I totally agree with this excerpt of the interview. The world is constantly changing; it is always shifting towards these 21st century based 'themes'. It was even my inspiration for writing this book, to show why middle schools need to be more 21st century based, and so this quote is something I believe to be completely valid.

In regards to what kids should be learning about programming, Hunt believes in teaching, "A basic understanding of sequential control, iteration, data and algorithms. It doesn't have to be complicated or in-depth. Beginner language and environments like Scratch, turtle graphics, etc., are a great place to start. You don't even need a computer for some learning - you can do 'turtle graphic' programming using fellow students.

Similar to having a giant, person-sized chessboard, where you tell people to go forward 3 squares, over 1, that sort of thing. That gives people the idea of sequential instructions, which is an important introductory concept. From a simple start like that, then some fun with Scratch to practice with basic logic and control; I'd then suggest a friendly but capable language such as Ruby. You can use that build anything from games to full-fledged commercial apps and websites."

A very interesting, new perspective as to starting small, by learning the concepts of computer science through beginner languages, and then moving forward to writing bigger and better programs.

When asked how the teachers should teach their students to code, Hunt brought up a point I had not considered. "Let them loose with the technology. Let the kids play with it. Fuel their natural curiosity. The nice thing about programming is that you can experiment to your heart's content without worrying about breaking anything. Digging around and messing with it is the best way to learn."

Obviously, this answer may not be what school district administration members are looking for, but it makes sense in the grand scheme of things. If you were to search on any platform or advice app for 'How do I learn to code?', some tutorials will be provided, but you'll soon notice that many people will talk about the need to do something, to create, and to not to blindly follow a tutorial. This is something that I also agree with, in that it is so valuable to get your feet wet in learning how to code.

Personally, I was so obsessed with following any tutorial I could find online, that when it came to actually trying to start a project, I failed miserably. But it turned out great, because it's what happens when most people attempt to make something for the first time; all you can do is continue to learn and build, and the more you do so, the more you succeed.

Finally, when asked about why so many kids are hesitant to learn and succeed in the coding environment, he commented, "I wish I knew. I think there are a couple of factors at play:

1) Most adults don't know how to code, and know nothing about it.

2) Most schools don't offer any classes or chances to learn to program.

3) Certain concepts might be hard to grasp at certain stages of development. For instance, your brain has to develop to a certain point before you can grasp the concept of a variable. So programming curriculum needs to take into account age-appropriate concepts.

4) Programming is perceived as "hard," when many kids would rather just play games. And yet, look at what some kids are doing in Minecraft, for example, using Redstone as a crude programming environment."

All of these are common occurrences that not only I have lived through personally, but many around me have as well. That is why it is so important to unveil these myths and to show people that the path to becoming a computer programmer is easier than may be perceived.

At the end of the day, Hunt provided some refreshingly new information, in following a stricter course of learning computer science aspects and letting kids run wild.

Ward Cunningham

Computer Science Expert and inventor of the Wiki Ward Cunningham had a lot to say about computer programming among youths.

Ward first dove into the importance for programs, especially with two scenarios.

Firstly, Cunningham remarked how he personally loves to read tons of different programs (not necessarily programming them yourself) in different languages. He enjoys reading them and then ascertaining what needs to be done, the method the programmer went about completing his task, really just dissecting all aspects of the program overall.

Secondly, in the field of coding, you'll often find yourself forced to work with a lot of different people on projects. In these types of scenarios, you will be forced to read programs, in order to accomplish what you need to get done.

Because of both of these scenarios, you have to learn how to read programs in languages you don't know. With diving into these foreign programs, you will have to ascertain what the main purpose of the function is, you will need to break down the parts of the program, and find what you don't know, in order to Google it, once the program is broken down. Similar to a conversationalist with linguistics, there is logic to programming, in that you need to be able to read and learn programs, even with many things you don't know. *All you should need to know with programs is how you can break it down into something you understand.*

Cunningham admitted that this is not something you can easily incorporate into a school's curriculum. Rather, it is more experiential for students, where you either learn to love the unknown or learn to hate what you don't understand.

Cunningham remarked that coding is, in a lot of ways, a lot like being an explorer, in that you need to be able to make progress even when everything is up in the air.

In regards to what computer programming language kids should learn, Cunningham remarked that what he thinks people want to accomplish is to make something that excites them, because this would then fuel their drive to continue their learning of programming. As we all know though, with the advent of the Internet and all of today's technological breakthroughs, that it is increasingly harder to do, so this part takes a bit of creativity on the part of both the student and the teacher.

Thus leads to Cunningham's personal story, where he attended a computer science summit where they were asked this question: what can we teach kids that could excite them, could wake these kids up?

Now, many suggested Arduino and Internet of Things programming. An Arduino is basically a small computer that can be utilized to wirelessly connect all of your home devices. The example I use with the Internet of Things is being able to turn the lights on in your house with your phone – it's all about connected devices and such.

An Arduino-based project is likely to excite young kids, because of the limitless project possibilities that arise. Arduinos are the type of hardware that can be utilized with everything from robots to self-driving cars to security systems. They are literally one of the many cores, both literally and figuratively, in order to link up anything and everything in the invisible 'web' that makes up the Internet of Things. Would you be excited if you could turn on a smoothie machine with an IPad? Probably.

When Cunningham was asked what he feel young kids should learn, he responded that kids should explore jQuery. JQuery is an older library, or a subset, of the JavaScript programing language. At that time, and even still today, the library, which was originally designed for animation (among other things), is used by all ability-levels, from novice to professional.

What he likes about it most, though, is that it has a surprising ability to it, in that it does many things you wouldn't expect it to do with its power over the page. Anyone can run jQuery, and change pages on the web in a way that is startling. Once students can learn the simple syntax (the grammar for coding) of jQuery, you can transform everything on the screen. You can have students learn and build off this to create something new, fresh, and exciting.

Another thing Cunningham likes about jQuery is that it only involves typing on a computer. In today's world, almost everyone has access to one, and gives the user real power over the browser, which Cunningham even called 'magical'.

However, when messing around with Arduinos, there's not a lot of power for the user's actions solely, as with these types of devices comes wiring, electrical support, and other complications on top of the code needed to make a program run. Thus, it seems like an illogical choice to choose Arduino and Internet of Things Programming for first time programmers, but rather utilize the jQuery library.

Additionally, when asked how young students should be taught to program, Cunningham opted for the 'cyclic approach'.

This approach entails completing a series of tiny little projects under one umbrella lesson plan. Each week, you would learn something new and expand your capabilities. He says that this cyclic experience is great, especially in regards to constantly building your knowledge base and applying what you previously learned week after week to make something new. After all, he says, great programmers are always making something new, going into something non-existent, and through application of current knowledge and the constant, cyclic increase of abilities, you are setting the tone for students overall success.

After talking about this, Cunningham then began discussing the "Learn to Code in an Hour" programs. There are a lot of these that are all a little obscure, but should be something that everyone should learn. These little exercises, the little games, teach you about coding in a fun and interactive way. However, he feels they miss one important thing that was just touched upon: computer programming is something where you're supposed to bring a world into an existence that didn't exist before.

Many of these programs have something similar to this scenario: "Here's the world I created for you, see if you can get the robot to move in my world." At the end of the day, you don't actually learn how to build a world from imagination to existence; as such, the representation in totality is a bit trivial, so a heavier premium needs to be focused on new creations, similar to the ability for which project-based learning is founded upon.

Brian Kernighan

Brian Kernighan is a brilliant man in the field of computer science; he helped to push forth the UNIX operating system and co-authored the first ever book about the C Programming language.

When asked his thoughts on young kids learning to code, Kernighan first mentioned how students should pursue programming only on the basis of interest. He remarked that teaching programming should not be a 'force fit', such as exhibited with other subjects in school like the mandatory Math and English courses.

He believes it's very important that kids learn to code by, "Just going off and doing it." He says how he loves teaching languages with lots of syntax and having students explore that language, and then adding algorithms and data structures later on. This way, it makes the learning less academic and more fun.

To further demonstrate his ideas, he talked about the heavily aforementioned Scratch programming language, where a large component of its success revolves around people going on the site, starting to play with it, and making anything. It doesn't necessarily matter what, but rather that you *do something.*

When he was younger, Kernighan went to the University of Toronto, where there weren't many languages to program in, and there weren't a large number of computers around to actually code on (there were only two in the whole university!). He firmly believes that it doesn't really matter what you're doing, or how you're doing it, but rather that you are actually doing something.

When asked the best way for kids to be taught, Kernighan had some great points.

He answered first with 'full control questions.' He believes that it is a bad idea to expose kids to only one programming language or program, and as such, teachers need to expose their students to many different languages and find a way to combine them in an assignment or two.

Then, he would have them writing interesting programs, revolving around something they care about. Overall, teachers should put students in an environment where students can learn about programming in a more holistic sense, then learn more formal structures (what does this program mean, what are the ways, how can this be made more efficient, etc.).

Another large part of teaching kids would be to ensure that the students programming would actually be able to talk about their program. Kernighan says, "To be able to communicate explanations of the program, of the parameters and uses, both orally and in the written, are so important." In reality, as also mentioned prior in the book, in whatever areas of life you may be concentrating on, writing and speaking are incredibly important. In this case, people need to be able to communicate their technical explanations.

Kernighan then went on to discuss the 2 courses he teachers each year: one in the fall and one in the spring, and how they relate to programming.

The spring course he taught is a 'junior level course'. In essence, it is a project-based-learning course, where most of what students learn is by going off and building something in a group. Over the semester, students would complete their respective projects (mostly phone apps or web services). With this course, most of what they learned is the direct result of being forced to understand how to go about completing the project, the techniques to do so, information with databases, working with the cloud, what language to use, and everything else under the sun.

These students would also get lectures every week from Kernighan, where he gives talks about different programming languages, exciting tools, and overall software engineering skills. At the end of the day, you learn by doing, and only apply some lecture knowledge in your project as necessary.

In the fall course, however, Kernighan teaches groups of non-technical students, a course intended for English and History majors. This greatly resembles that of a potential course for middle school students, considering that a large majority of the class would have little experience in computer programming.

In this class, he says, most students are afraid of technology, math and arithmetic. To combat the fears, he teaches a lot of the fundamentals of our world's technology. He goes over what computers do, how they do it, binary bits, software systems, operating systems, apps, and a tiny bit of JavaScript, as well as how the internet works, internet privacy, and internet security. That's a lot! The course overall is aimed at providing information about the technology in our lives.

Additionally, these students receive problem sets each week to learn where they test their knowledge of the material.

The students would go off to labs and make web pages. A fair amount is learned from the labs, considering that the students are able to apply their understanding from the lectures.

Now, this may seem like an ideal solution to teaching programming in middle school; however, Kernighan is hesitant to take the same approach of the Fall Course as with middle school students. His main reason for this is that the reward structures would be very different for middle schools; his students complete the labs for credit, while middle school kids would work to try to learn and advance.

He offered an alternate solution, in that middle schools should try to make a less formal, organized version of the Fall Program, with group work. Overall, Kernighan's experience and knowledge for middle school students was limited, but he provided excellent insight into the overall nature of coding and provided a great potential plan.

Conclusion

At the end of the day, what will separate those who are succeeding on the frontier and those hit by the harsh conditions of computer illiteracy will be computer science, and all related teachings. This is why computer science needs to be taught, especially in middle schools all across the country.

CHAPTER 10

Entrepreneurship

Before we go any further, let's clear the air. In my mind, as it has been shaped by my environment, Entrepreneurship doesn't have to imply starting your own business. It doesn't have to mean quitting your job to focus on your company. It doesn't mean spending your life chasing after that business idea you've always wanted to see grow and prosper. No, it's not any of that.

In my opinion, entrepreneurship is one of the most valuable skills today. Period. The ability to think for yourself, to solve problems, to even utilize other skills in this book is more important than most of what is taught in Middle School. As such, I think they need to start teaching it in middle school.

I consider myself to be an entrepreneur, and I have been one since I was about 13. I have a heavy background in entrepreneurship; not in the traditional sense, but in a modified way. Over the course of my life, I have started or been part of many real businesses.

When I was about 7 years old, I first started "Aaron & Austin's Sport Business", a company designed to sell all types of sports cards. This endeavor was quite successful; I estimated that I must've made about $300.

Since then, I've tried (and failed) to succeed at starting an edible aluminum foil company, on the basis that I couldn't actually make the product. Same story with a Digital Marketing firm, as I realized that I knew almost nothing about digital marketing (I was only trying to copy my brother's digital marketing business). Then I tried to get sponsors for my brother's conference, Next Gen Summit, which I failed at miserably as well.

Yes, I failed at all three; but I learned more than I ever could in regards to life through these endeavors in entrepreneurship. And that's important too.

My Backstory

The first time, it was the fall of 9th grade, and my brother Justin was on a gap year from college, and at the time, I was bored and money hungry. One day, Justin came home from a meeting and told me about how he was going to this local Shark Tank-like competition at a local college, and was going to 'pitch' his higher education consulting firm to the panel of 3 judges, in hopes of winning the grand prize. He asked me to go along with him, to pitch any idea; to do nothing in particular, but rather just to get a taste of what this might be like.

I decided to go, and pitch an idea of mine I had long thought of: edible aluminum foil for your sandwiches, burritos, and Paninis. No name, no product, no nothing really. But what I did have was an idea and a positive attitude. So I decided to give it a shot. Fast forward a few days, and I'm at the competition. I'm the youngest kid there by two years, and I don't know what I'm going to say. No biggie, right? Well, I get up there, I make a huge fool of myself by being absurd, and I crushed it! To this day, it might rank among one of my favorite speeches, in that my entire presentation consisted of 1% content and 99% jokes.

But it turned out well. One of the judges created a new award for me on the spot, paying me $100, which helped cover a few Chipotles. It was "Project Research," as I call it. I also received a free one-month pass at a local "launch pad", an entrepreneurial hub of sorts. He said it would help me get my idea off the ground, and I was really stoked about it.

The next judge I spoke to was a cool and quiet guy, who said, "Get this off the ground, and I'll give you the keys to my house." At this point, I didn't have another care in the world.

Finally, the last judge I spoke to was an experienced professional in the food industry, who specialized in healthy and edible snacks. She told me that she had a few contacts in that industry, some chefs that she would love me to speak to, and actually help get my idea off of the ground! She gave me her card, and I was excited to continue our dialogue!

Here, my first real company was birthed, which I called eFOIL. Now, I was seriously interested in doing this for a long time, but I ended up not having the time or the resources to explore further. Throughout my whole endeavor with eFOIL, though, I learned one of the most important things in business, because it was something I did not do: Follow-Up.

Follow up is an extremely important thing to do, in every aspect of life. I just didn't realize it until too late. It just never came to me that taking advantage of resources that were willing and able to assist you was a smart move. You could really get advice at any time and from anywhere, from someone whom you had just met and wanted to give you advice, or someone who was willing to fund your project. At the end of the day, follow up is crucial to success, and in my mind, it was the main reason this venture never really took off.

The next story comes with the Next Gen Summit, the conference I had been planning with Justin, my brother, which I touched upon earlier. I had tried to obtain monetary sponsors for this first time event, and was failing critically. However, one day, I received an email from one of the company's I had reached out to, saying that they were willing to discuss a potential proposition over the phone. It was a fairly large company, who had just been bought by Intel for over $100 million dollars only a short while before. I was going to be speaking with one of their Directors of Marketing, someone who could potentially sponsor our event.

Justin let me take the lead on the call. This was the first time where I would be the one pitching. I was so scared; I did the research, I practiced what I was going to say, I thought of potential sound bites that could help sway this man. I tried to do my very best to impress my brother, and to succeed at my task.

We took this call in our cozy little piano room, where my brother was sitting next to me on this call. We made our introductions, made some small talk, and then got into it. We talked about their company, what they could do, etc. Unfortunately, from right off the bat, the guy wasn't going for it. I couldn't see it, but my brother did though, which is why he never interrupted me nor tried to help me; he saw this as a good learning experience, he told me later.

It got to a point in the conversation where the guy flat-out said, "I simply don't know how this can work." Now, the worst part of the story comes with how I responded. I tried to counter with a line that was so mean and inaccurate that I single-handedly lost the already-failing proposition. "Well, no one really knows about you, and we can change that."

Yes, I basically said to a marketing officer of a company that had just been sold to Intel for more money than I might ever make that no one knew about their company.

I know, it was a pretty bad move. But I learned more in those 10 seconds than I ever could by studying from a textbook.

I learned two things: first, *you can't try to undo the damage that has already been done.* After I just insulted this man, I tried to cover it up, stuttering that I meant it in regards to their social media, as my brother's face turned a bright red.

However I now know that instead of trying to cover it up, the only possible thing to do there was apologize. But, there shouldn't be a need to apologize, which leads me into the second thing I learned: *It's OK to stop.* In life, on a call, in an interview, wherever. The circumstances surrounding the situation have no importance. The only thing that does matter is that you should take a second to breathe, rather of saying something stupid.

That was one thing that I wish I would've known, so I wouldn't have insulted the guy. It's perfectly natural to take a second, collect yourself, and move on with what you're doing. Hopefully, you'll take that second in the future so you don't make the mistake I did.

Finally, my last mistake came starting in the spring of the same year (it was a busy 9th grade), where I tried to start and grow Sapphire Designs, a full service Digital Marketing company. The basis for this was that I saw how my brother could succeed, and I wanted to emulate him. He had started a full service Digital marketing agency just a few months before, and I just wanted to copy him and to make some money. But I failed miserably.

The biggest thing I learned from this company: *Find a niche, and conquer it.* At 14 years old, I tried to step into a field with thousands upon thousands of competitors, trying to succeed as a small fish in a huge pond. After failing, after getting no clients because nobody wanted to trust a 'stupid' 14 year old, I realized that there was no point trying to compete in a field that was already pre-existing for a great number of years, against people with more skill and experience than I had at the time.

The biggest thing that came out of this for me was to understand that the chance of success in a small-fish-big-pond scenario is so miniscule. Rather, you would be much better off starting a business in your untapped market, and finding success there. Yes, you can start a business in any field; however, your success may vary based on what type of pond you are trying to survive in, as well as the pre-existing fish in that market.

Now, I learned so much more than that over the years, but honestly, who has time for that many stories? But these three pieces of knowledge I collected through real-life experiences. I failed, yes. But we can all laugh at our failures, or we can learn from them, and use them all to our advantage as things to learn from. Overall, I equate my success in life today to a long list of things; but one of the biggest is that I learned from experience with entrepreneurship.

But again, I'm going to say it, and I can't stress it enough; I'm not saying that it has to be with a business. Rather, it comes with solving any problem any capacity in everyday life; with this, real life experience can surely teach you more than any textbook. I stake my reputation on that.

Student Beliefs

Many students agreed with me in that they felt Entrepreneurship was something important to have. They remarked how successful entrepreneurs start early, and how schools should encourage youth entrepreneurship.

Students believed that entrepreneurship should be incorporated into the curriculum for a lot of different reasons. For example, one student remarked how entrepreneurship equates to a more creative mindset. They said this could also impact what results teachers can see in the classroom, potentially accounting for overall success of any student. For me, an entrepreneurship-based lifestyle led to an increased ability for me to solve problems, which I believe is the foundation of entrepreneurship.

After I started to delve into entrepreneurship, my ability to succeed in my courses that required creative problem solving, such as math, greatly increased. This was because of my experience in problem solving itself, a positive effect of being an entrepreneur (they say that an entrepreneur's number one asset is always his brain). This alone branches into a variety of different ways for success, which just proves that Entrepreneurship is incredibly important to learn / be implemented in the curriculum.

Likewise, as part of entrepreneurship, many develop a skill to take an idea and convince people that it's a good idea. *The Good Ol' Art of Persuasion.* This can apply beyond school, as the ability to persuade people to buy your product or believe in your ideas is a large component of life. It's involved in everything from sales to research papers to arguing with your teacher about losing points on a test! A full implementation of entrepreneurship can lead to successful argument construction, thus allowing a student to succeed in a multitude of different ways.

Additionally, students felt it was important to learn entrepreneurship because it provides the opportunity for kids to branch out of normal curriculum and straying away from the traditional education 'path'.

Most don't think teaching something as crazy as entrepreneurship should be a priority. Many think that middle school is a joke, where many of the kids in the schools are 'too young to have any freedom'. Well frankly, not having entrepreneurship courses deny students the opportunity they deserve.

On a similar note, many feel that teachers don't have the mindset to teach entrepreneurship, specifically because they don't have the mindset that teaching students a skill they could use outside of school could be important. Many teachers only want to stick to the curriculum at hand, especially in regards to state tests. They don't think it's important to prepare students for life outside the middle school classroom.

I think it's something they should teach, or at least provide a foundation for. It could even potentially inspire students for later in their schooling. Teaching entrepreneurship would be a great thing for kids looking to pursue these careers, and unfortunately, schools are just not providing the necessary opportunities, even if there are kids willing to make the extra effort.

Teaching Entrepreneurship

Now, there are many options of how to implement the teaching of entrepreneurship.

Firstly, I believe that the teachings of entrepreneurship, and business in general, should be discussed in my aforementioned one mandatory class period, where students will experience new, exciting, hands-on learning about business, financial literacy, and many more 21st century life skills. I feel that the possibility of discussing the concept of businesses themselves, how businesses actually function, and the structure of a company could help to provide a basic foundation of a student's knowledge of entrepreneurship. This is something that could easily help students succeed in the world of business at a young age, which is necessary for practically every walk of life.

However, many students have proposed that even something smaller, such as an elective or even just an after school program as a collaborative interface for entrepreneurial success would allow students to obtain more knowledge about the subject.

Additionally, something that has crossed my mind for a while is the idea of every middle school student starting their own business or solving their own problem in an extremely small entrepreneurial hub or startup accelerator, that only has to be big enough so students can see success and can truly learn.

This type of program, though complex, would help to promote and teach entrepreneurship. After all, the best method of learning is the hands-on approach, especially with entrepreneurship, so why can't students get their proverbial feet wet? What I envision this program to be is a stepping-stone for students to practice real-life skills in all walks of life.

In this program, students would first take time to analyze the world around them, and obtain a sense of problems on any scale that need to be fixed. After, students would come up with their best problems that would need to be solved; they would then pick one idea to work with, and in groups of 3-5, endeavor at entrepreneurial success.

They would have extended periods of time to work on their product, or service. They would create the idea and follow up with it, market it, 'pitch' it to investors, and everything else under the sun. They would really just endeavor at creating their own first company or solve their first problem, something that shows students what the real world is like, to see what is necessary to succeed in that sort of environment.

Yes, this idea might be outrageous, expensive, and non-helpful to some; but to most, I feel that this opportunity might be a gateway towards success with this essential skill, to provide opportunity through a simulation for real life success. And all the while, you might actually get some great ideas accomplished and some problems solved.

Current Models

Now, I'm not the only one who believes that entrepreneurship is an essential skill.

Babson College is a university located in Massachusetts that, according to U.S News & World Report, has an undergraduate school ranked #1 for entrepreneurship, *for eighteen consecutive times.* They have specialized programs that are designed to obtain entrepreneurial success for students selected into the unique program. Top Experts design these incredible programs, and their goal involves, "Preparing leaders to impact the world through entrepreneurial thought and action."

I learned about the school's programs through a relative, and was immediately fascinated by the incredibility of the entrepreneurship program. According to their website, "Babson provides a unique opportunity for entrepreneurs and aspiring entrepreneurs to explore a world full of opportunities and new pathways to success. In today's environment of uncertainty, the world needs entrepreneurial solutions and leaders who create great economic and social value everywhere. Babson teaches principles of Entrepreneurial Thought and Action® that can be applied to new ventures, growing companies, family businesses, and large corporations." Sounds familiar, right?

Their specific programs are one- to two-week transformational learning experiences for select groups of entrepreneurial leaders from across the world, where participants learn from and are trained by faculty at the No. 1 institution in the world for entrepreneurship education. Babson also consults closely with partnering institutions to ensure that programs meet the unique goals of the participants.

Babson Entrepreneurship Programs are also blended-learning experiences. In addition to having large amounts of classroom time to focus on entrepreneurial learning, the programs feature a variety of hands-on experiences that are intensive, group-oriented, and interactive. They may include business simulations, guest speakers, visits to companies, field trips, and other off-campus activities."

These programs are quite unique, and provide a very exciting opportunity for those interested in entrepreneurship lives, creating one heck of a program to encompass everything necessary to succeed with this skill in today's world.

Overall, after finding out about the school, I am officially obsessed with Babson College. Honestly, their beliefs are so in line with what I have been trying to say, it's practically crazy. For more information, definitely check out Babson.edu, and I encourage you to explore their awesome programs.

Expert Opinions

Matt Krisiloff

Matt Krisiloff manages the new fellowship program at Y Combinator, one of the most prestigious venture capital firms in the world, with investments in companies like Reddit, Airbnb, Dropbox, and Stripe, which have all been valued at over $50 billion (https://www.cbinsights.com/blog/y-combinator-startup-valuation/), just to name a few. For the full, incredibly lengthy and shockingly successful list, head over to yclist.com.

Matt runs the YC Fellowship department, a new endeavor from the venture capital firm at increasing the entrepreneurial spirit. "[The] YC Fellowship is an 8 week experiment we're running from mid-September to mid-November [of 2015]. It will be like a lighter version of YC for idea and prototype stage companies. Each startup will receive a $12k equity-free grant, as well as advice from YC partners. The program will be less intensive than YC, but we're still going to try to help teams a lot. For the duration of the program, teams will work with YC partners for office hours, have access to YC resources like AWS and Microsoft credits, and have kickoff and end events in Mountain View."

This idea-stage-centered program allows for an incredible amount of new startups to receive the funding and resources necessary to grow their extremely new companies. And Matt manages it all.

When asked what he looked for in accepting people into YC Fellowship, as well as for good entrepreneurs in general, he said among the best signs were determination. Being able to have a mindset that you'll make it whatever you're working on happen. Likewise, being passionate about one's idea, and being flexible enough to change the direction of where you're going if needed are important. There are many other characteristics, he said, but these are the ones at the top of the list.

Now, when asked how anyone can learn to be entrepreneurial, Matt gave some advice in that the best way to do so is to start working on an idea for a while. Now, that doesn't necessarily mean starting a startup, especially just for the sake of doing it – that's a big pain for nothing. Matt reflected on how he had worked on a company of his for about a year and a half, and how it was hard, but he learned from it.

He also pointed out how people today are incredibly lucky, as we are all living at a time where people can share good ideas. Through blog posts, twitter, and other forms of social media and communication, Average Joes can adhere to the advice of the likes of Paul Graham, Sam Altman, Peter Thiel, Fred Wilson, Chris Dickson, and Mark Andreessen, just to name a few. He says that you can learn a lot by going around and reading what these founders have to say, something that I couldn't agree more with.

Now, when asked, "Should all young people be entrepreneurs?" Matt answered with a resounding No.

He said that he personally doesn't think everyone can do it, as it's an incredibly hard thing to do. The amount of hard work that needs to be put in with a startup is probably not something that most could undertake in, considering the low success rate of many of these companies.

However, he did agree that he thinks it can be helpful to develop an entrepreneurial mindset. He feels that one track-type of personality generally results from an entrepreneurial lifestyle, a good track-type at that, and that the different experiences people have lead to different, equally great mindsets. Also, Matt talked about how a good approach in the entrepreneurial field is to become an early employee at a company, and as such, to get a great stake in that business. And then at that business, you can apply the entrepreneurial mindset to achieve in that company. It's practically a win-win.

Paul Graham

My idol, Paul Graham, also had a little to say on the subject. That company I mentioned earlier, that Matt runs one of the programs for, Y Combinator? He founded it. Paul was also gracious enough to put this interview on his website, so feel free to check it out here: http://www.paulgraham.com/int15.html.

What Makes A Good Entrepreneur

When asked what makes a good entrepreneur, I was given the greatest answer: "An entrepreneur is someone who starts their own business. But only a tiny fraction of new businesses are startups. I don't know much about entrepreneurship generally, but I know about startup founders. To be a good startup founder you must above all be determined. But be flexible as well. Startups do not, as a rule, plow through obstacles. They have to go around them. Sometimes to the extent of re-defining the playing field so that the obstacle is no longer in the way. The short version of what a startup founder needs to be is 'relentlessly resourceful.'

I'm not involved with selecting startups for Y Combinator anymore, but that is certainly what they are trying to find."

Very profound words, I have to say.

All Young People Should Explore

Additionally, when asked if all young people should be entrepreneurs, he interpreted the question in that, "I'm going to continue to assume that by entrepreneurs you mean startup founders, and the answer to that is an emphatic no. Most people are not suited to it. I'd be surprised if more than 1% of people are. And even for those few, it's a mistake to start too young. If a startup succeeds, it takes over your life in a way that cuts off lots of other opportunities. It's a mistake to do that sort of pruning before you understand what you're losing by it.

I wouldn't advise people to try to start startups before about 23. Before that you should be exploring."

This is very similar to what I have mentioned, and I couldn't agree more. Additionally, the keyword to point out here is exploring. Young kids need to find their way into entrepreneurship through exploration of the field, and one potential way to do so is with the aforementioned program. *To learn through experience.* Also, associated with this, Graham mentioned that in regards to learning entrepreneurship and developing an entrepreneurial mindset, 'The best way is by doing it. Nothing will teach you about startups like starting one. The next best thing would be to observe an existing startup in action.'

Overall, the legendary Paul Graham excellent entrepreneurial advice that I completely agree with.

Additionally, while on the subject of what makes up an Entrepreneur, Entrepreneurs in general need so many different characteristics and have to possess unusual traits that complement each other in such a mystical way that it just works. In October of 2010, Paul Graham outlined 5 of these perfectly in one of the heaviest-impact essay I have ever had the opportunity to read, and I felt it is a perfect addition to this section of the book. When I was first exploring my entrepreneurial lifestyle, this was the first real advice I took. Pulled from his personal website at paulgraham.com (which is also available as a Forbes article) here are the five fundamentals for entrepreneurial success:

1. Determination

This has turned out to be the most important quality in startup founders. We thought when we started Y Combinator that the most important quality would be intelligence. That's the myth in the Valley. And certainly you don't want founders to be stupid. But as long as you're over a certain threshold of intelligence, what matters most is determination. You're going to hit a lot of obstacles. You can't be the sort of person who gets demoralizedeasily.

Bill Clerico and Rich Aberman of WePay are a good example. They're doing a finance startup, which means endless negotiations with big, bureaucratic companies. When you're starting a startup that depends on deals with big companies to exist, it often feels like they're trying to ignore you out of existence. But when Bill Clerico starts calling you, you may as well do what he asks, because he is not going away.

2. Flexibility

You do not however want the sort of determination implied by phrases like "don't give up on your dreams." The world of startups is so unpredictable that you need to be able to modify your dreams on the fly. The best metaphor I've found for the combination of determination and flexibility you need is a running back. He's determined to get downfield, but at any given moment he may need to go sideways or even backwards to get there.

The current record holder for flexibility may be Daniel Gross of Greplin. He applied to YC with some bad ecommerce idea. We told him we'd fund him if he did something else. He thought for a second, and said ok. He then went through two more ideas before settling on Greplin. He'd only been working on it for a couple days when he presented to investors at Demo Day, but he got a lot of interest. He always seems to land on his feet.

3. Imagination

Intelligence does matter a lot of course. It seems like the type that matters most is imagination. It's not so important to be able to solve predefined problems quickly as to be able to come up with surprising new ideas. In the startup world, most good ideasseem bad initially. If they were obviously good, someone would already be doing them. So you need the kind of intelligence that produces ideas with just the right level of craziness.

Airbnb is that kind of idea. In fact, when we funded Airbnb, we thought it was too crazy. We couldn't believe large numbers of people would want to stay in other people's places. We funded them because we liked the founders so much. As soon as we heard they'd been supporting themselves by selling Obama and McCain branded breakfast cereal, they were in. And it turned out the idea was on the right side of crazy after all.

4. Naughtiness

Though the most successful founders are usually good people, they tend to have a piratical gleam in their eye. They're not Goody Two-Shoes type good. Morally, they care about getting the big questions right, but not about observing proprieties. That's why I'd use the word naughty rather than evil. They delight inbreaking rules, but not rules that matter. This quality may be redundant though; it may be implied by imagination.

Sam Altman of Loopt is one of the most successful alumni, so we asked him what question we could put on the Y Combinator application that would help us discover more people like him. He said to ask about a time when they'd hacked something to their advantage—hacked in the sense of beating the system, not breaking into computers. It has become one of the questions we pay most attention to when judging applications.

5. Friendship

Empirically it seems to be hard to start a startup with

just one founder. Most of the big successes have two or three. And the relationship between the founders has to be strong. They must genuinely like one another, and work well together. Startups do to the relationship between the founders what a dog does to a sock: if it can be pulled apart, it will be.

Emmett Shear and Justin Kan of Justin.tv are a good example of close friends who work well together. They've known each other since second grade. They can practically read one another's minds. I'm sure they argue, like all founders, but I have never once sensed any unresolved tension between them."

An incredible piece of writing, if I do say so myself, in that five totally opposite parts of life can come together to create an entrepreneur.

At the end of the day, one thing is for sure: Paul Graham knows his stuff about entrepreneurship.

Conclusion

What would the world be like if everyone thought and behaved like an entrepreneur? The possibilities would be endless, with an incredibly positive effect on the world. Let's try to get there, and take the first step in doing so: implementing the teaching of entrepreneurship courses in middle schools.

CHAPTER 11

Final Thoughts
On Education

T he following three pieces are from three different educational experts, who each had something incredible and different to say about education as a whole.

Alan Kay

Alan Kay is arguably one of the most successful programmers I've ever had the opportunity to interview. According to his Wikipedia page, "Alan Curtis Kay is an American computer scientist. He has been elected a Fellow of the American Academy of Arts and Sciences, the National Academy of Engineering, and the Royal Society of Arts." He is also someone with a more extensive work background than can possibly be imagined.

Kay is also the president at an organization known as Viewpoints Research, an organization incorporated in 2001 to improve 'powerful ideas education' for the world's children and to advance the state of systems research and personal computing. Many of our themes co-evolved with the inventions of networked personal computers, graphical user interfaces and dynamic object-oriented programming."

When Mr. Kay, who I interviewed over email, responded with his answers to my questions, he mainly focused on one body of writing, which he had ironically enough already entitled 'Unorthodox'. It goes as follows:

"When we learn a musical instrument we are investing time and energy both into *now* and into *later*. We want to play *now*, and we also want to learn for *later* to play better and deeper. A good musical curriculum and musical helpers will make this happen. Similarly for sports: we want both *now*, and *later*, and a good sports program will facilitate this.

Schools on the other hand have traditionally been aimed only at *later* and only provide for *now* considerable practice but very little actual *play*. This quite misses the point of how we humans have been set up by nature.

Another difficulty with "school" that is important to think about is that it is supposed to teach certain subjects - like reading and writing and mathematics - to all, regardless of whether the students are interested or want to learn them. This is a huge contrast with the arts and sports, which are almost always voluntary electives.

I happen to believe in two quite contradictory things in education: that choice and personal motivation are "all important"—*and* that bringing the next generation up in the strongest ideas produced by a civilization is "all important". The first belief is that a personal connection with "richness" of experience and the choices of what and how are part of what makes life worth living. The second belief is that our societal ways of cooperating and reasonably examining many sides of important issues requires us to learn how to think and act a lot better than our genetic heritage alone is set up for. We can think of this as a basic important tension between what people *want* and what they *need*.

One way to deal with contradictory ideas is to think of them as not being made of "matter" - where they can't occupy the same space - but as made from "light" - we can shine spots of light in the same space and they happily coexist because radiation superposes.

This idea is the basic principle in *design*: to be able hold mutually incompatible ideas in one's head for a long time without trying to resolve them. Another way to look at this is that "design" is even more about "problem finding" than "problem solving". Current day schooling has real difficulties with this idea: it is mostly about getting students to solve problems rather than to find them.

More than 100 years ago Maria Montessori - a first rate genius in a number of areas, including medicine, anthropology and education - had a deep insight about children and learning. She noticed that we are all driven by our genetics to learn the culture around us as "reality" and this drive is especially strong in children. Especially important is that the desire to become acculturated dominates individual preference. We see this often in the small in children with musical or sports oriented parents winding up learning the music and the sports as a matter of course. When an environment is total we don't think about making choices: we just acclimate.

We see this in the large in many areas of life. But we don't see it for (say) mathematics because most adults don't know mathematics, and thus the children won't see mathematics as part of the culture. We can see that getting something really new into the general culture might take hundreds of years, if it happens at all. Montessori realized that if a school was created that embodied *as culture* what she wanted the children to learn, then there was a great chance that the learning would happen without the children feeling the pain of having choice taken away from them.

The next step in thinking about how to do this is to realize that *culture* means *now*. That is, it is what is going on constantly around us that we take as our environment, and that is what we are driven to accommodate ourselves to.

Seymour Papert realized that mathematics could be put into the *now* for most people via certain kinds of interactive programming on a personal computer in the form of the Logo programming language. Now the computer starts to feel more like a musical instrument, and the mathematics more like music that can be played in the *now*, and that one can get much better at for *later*. Create a culture - he called it "MathLand" - where people can live and play, and all will start to learn math for very different reasons than being told to. He made an analogy between how hard it is to learn French in a class in the US vs going to live in France for a few years.

Papert's approach was wonderful because he wanted everyone to get in contact with and internalize "Powerful Ideas", and he was able to design a computer environment that embodied some of the Powerful Ideas.

The first Powerful Idea is that there are Powerful Ideas (for example: agriculture, writing, calculus, democracy, equal rights, etc.) Another Powerful idea is the idea of debugging: that you can attempt much more ambitious goals if you can set up processes to find errors and correct them. A balancing Powerful Idea is that "design and vision" are what makes debugging really work: it is hard to debug a lump of clay into something beautiful - you need to have something beautiful in mind that gives rise to forms that can then be debugged, etc.

This leads to thinking about larger Powerful Ideas. For example, it is quite clear that we humans have "bad brains" - we are terrible thinkers. Francis Bacon in 1620 identified a few of the reasons: we are genetically poor thinkers with limited capacities and we rely on common sense and stories rather than real thinking; we are culturally poor thinkers (most of what most cultures believe is quite untrue); our languages are poor at representing ideas; and our academics and teachers persist in strenuously teaching bad old ideas. He called for the invention of "science" as a set of methods that would allow us to get beyond our error-full thinking (rather like many of the error-correcting processes of today to remove "noise" from communications media - Bacon wanted to remove "noise" from our thinking processes). Science is the most powerful invention our species has come up with in its 200,000 years on the planet.

But "actual science" is essentially not taught in K-12 schools. What is taught are some of the findings of science, but not what it is and how it is really done. And these teachings are usually restricted to the simpler areas of Physics, Chemistry and Biology, rather than to realize that it is *all* of our thought that needs these error-correcting processes.

For example, let's take the Powerful Idea that the actual knowledge of Science is found in the *negotiation* between "what's out there?" (the phenomena that we can detect) and the ways we have to represent what we think the phenomena mean. Can you see that this one-step-removed definition both opened the wonders of the last 400 years *and* gives us ways to think better about most things, including society, rights, governance, resources, and literally: our future?

Another Powerful Idea - that goes right alongside that of Science - is that the strongest representation system we've been able to invent in 200,000 years is the computer. It both includes all other representation systems, and goes qualitatively beyond them. It's the best way today to get our negotiations about our ways of knowing closer to what is likely to be going on.

So it's not just Papert's "MathLand" that we need to make and live in. We need "RealThinkingLand".

It's important to notice about simple logic that it is built from the ideas of "true" and "false", and this works well inside a sealed environment that does not refer to the outside. This is what mathematics is actually all about: being consistent in how implications can be made. Trying to use this reasoning system in the real world is misleading and dangerous. Why? Because in the real world we can't completely nail down our premises, we can't completely define our operations, and thus we can't completely rely on our results. Failure to understand this had led to some of the greatest disasters in history, all of which have been perfectly rationalized by the perpetrators using bad thinking.

Mathematics existed when Bacon proclaimed the need for Science. What he wanted was something *bigger than math*, in which mathematical kinds of reasoning could be used safely. And this is what Science does. Its system of logic is not made from "true" or "false" but from thousands of gradations of "false", some of them very powerful. The premises are not perfect, the operations are not perfect, the results are not perfect, but by checking all parts constantly against "what's out there?" greater reasoning than we have ever been able to do can now be done.

And this is how computers are used in Science today, and how their results are thought about.

This is a very powerful set of ideas, and I think you can see - especially with the mess the world is in when it doesn't have to be - that all people need this kind of thinking desperately."

Overall, his writing is too good to be summarized, and his thoughts something that I whole-heartedly agree with.

After Kay provided me with this information, he then answered my questions:

Q: What are your thoughts on young kids learning to code?
A: "Children should start to learn these ideas as early as possible including the new "reading and writing" of these ideas using the computer as a medium of expression."

Q: What do you feel should be taught in regards to kids learning how to code?
A: "What should be taught should be along the lines of the discussion above."

Q: What do you feel the best way to teach kids how to learn is?
A: "The best way to teach children to learn is to make a world they can live in that embodies the ideas and processes to be learned, just as our language is embodied in our current culture. Some of this world can be made in the computer, and some of it has to be made in our societal world."

Q: Why do you think so many people are hesitant to learn to code, when it is such an incredible opportunity?
A: "Most people do not do things just because they are a good idea. We are primarily set up to gauge our actions by what others do (that is part of being a social animal). Most people will wait until others are doing something. You can see that this can take decades or more."

Q: Do you feel logic is an important part of a curriculum that should be implemented in middle schools?
A: "'Logic' is hugely important, but neither classical Aristotelian logic nor mathematical logic is enough. These are dangerous and need the larger system of Science in order to do better thinking."

Q: Is there anything else that isn't taught to young students that you wish would be incorporated into the material?
A: "We need to help children learn all the stuff mentioned above, and a lot more!"

Jay McTighe

Jay McTighe has one of the best minds involved with education reform today. According to his website, "An experienced educator and noted author, Jay McTighe provides consulting services to schools, districts, regional service agencies and state departments of education." Already a mouthful – but you won't believe his brilliance until you hear his thoughts on education.

When asked about his original thoughts on education, McTighe immediately remarked that his thoughts aren't necessarily original, but he did specify that they most certainly aren't the norm in education today.

In a world in which the generation of youths today can access much of all of the world's knowledge on their smartphones, education should be prepared so that people can be increasingly able to evaluate what they find online, on print news, and through the media. Here, they can use the things they are learning in ways that will help them navigate the 'quick-changing world', instead of just memorizing information that already can be accessed quickly and being placed on a test. Additionally, education should prepare students to become creative problem solvers, to learn in teams, and again, not to go over the 'static information' learned today. In today's world, there is a great need to develop critical thinking, problem solving, and teamwork sills; in fact, he remarked that the need for this has never been greater!

Now, McTighe broke up his thoughts into three main 'chunks' of education.

With the first chunk, he discussed how it is extremely important for society to think about the goals of education. Education is not necessarily just about the static bodies of knowledge that come in textbooks for state tests. Rather, we need a dynamic concept of what education should be about in order to succeed in this filed.

McTighe's second chunk involved discussing what we know about meaningful and engaged learning.

Some lessons in school are going to be engaging, and excite students to the point where they would love to learn more, and other lessons are going to be extremely boring, regardless of the difficulty of the lesson. Some of McTighe's work is to remind some educators of learning qualities, in that teachers and administration should strive to have students looking forward to going to school, and not being bored. Here, McTighe gave a solution to this of education in workshops, where students can think about high-engagement lessons, share with one another, and generalize. Additionally, when McTighe utilized this method of teaching in a 'sample study', he found that this workshop-type method gets an incredibly positive result, with sample feedback including responses like authentic, real-life problem learning (not textbook work), the learning was challenging but worthwhile, some creative thinking was involved, interesting way to produce a product with control instead of doing exactly what the teacher demanded, getting to work with others with collaboration, received feedback as they were working. These are just some characteristics of the lesson people mentioned, consistent even with age, said McTighe. All in all, this sample study shows how schools can be so much better if we try to implement a lesson-style like this often.

In regards to his second chunk, McTighe also discussed how in his own work, he has to try to help educators, parents, and politicians alike understand that what was the norm when they went to school may not be appropriate today. We need clear modern goals for education and we need to be mindful of what meaningful and engaging learning looks like.

Now, for the grand finale. McTighe's third chunk is all about why schools are the way that they are, which he has concluded is due to sates and the federal government placing a premium on standardized tests, which greatly affects the modernization of school.

McTighe, who had been in education for quite some time, elaborated how over 20 years, he had watched over the growth of the number of standardized tests given out, and also the priority and pressures that the test results can have on schools, districts, and communities. Often, he says, real estate prices in areas are even directly correlated with school test scores, because parents who can afford it want to have their children attend 'premier' schools, where the only measure of the schools greatness is its standardized testing scores.

In addition, he shared how he believes that the scores themselves impact schools and school districts. He provided an example of how a superintendent in a 'failing' district may be fired, like with a business losing money. With no growth, schools go down, and then districts need to find a new leader. Standardized test scores, McTighe says, are costing principles their jobs, can affect the pay grade of a teaching staff and administration, and there are even some cases where if schools' test scores are too low, they will be 'reconstituted'. These schools will be closed, with all teachers fired with no guarantee of a rehire, and then opening up another school under a different name.

Over the last twenty years, there have been a growing number of standardized tests that students are forced to take, and the high stakes that students are pressured with has grown right along with it.

Now, how does this relate to middle schools and it's teaching?

Here's where it gets *juicy*. McTighe shared how he meets an incredible amount of teachers and educators over the country, many of whom would love to make school more 21st century based (oh, what a great thought!). However, these educators feel that they simply cannot change their curriculum, for fear that their schools and their jobs are being judged by how well kids perform on standardized tests. Like how the tail lags behind the dog, in this scenario, McTighe equated the tail to standardized tests, and the lagging dog to education.

Because tests are so important with the judging of the district, the influence test scores have, and how the media, particularly newspapers, love to share the latest insight about school districts, then educators have to take these testing factors seriously, and prepare the students for the tests. These educators feel as if they need to cover all the material for student readiness, and that because most standardized tests are multiple choice, often, critical thinking is not needed, thus resulting in a sole need to pick a right answer from many options, rather than using your brain to figure something out. This overall translates into educators teaching lots of content so that the instruction of students is broad and multiple choice based.

Often with this type of scenario, we see teachers teaching the requirements of the topic at hand, and then a large part of the unit would comprise of Test Prep, with lots of practice for multiple choice test taking. Now, McTighe says, this is incredibly 'wrong-headed', because multiple-choice questions simply aren't important in the grand scheme of things. For example, when we think about the important topics of argument construction, idea sharing, solving of complex problems with creative thinking, and working with others are nowhere to be found on multiple-choice tests. What he sees happening is that the things that are most important and are the greatest needs for skills in the 21st century are things that aren't tested, and as such, kids can't learn it. Teachers need to teach what's on the test, so that kids can do well, instead of the modern thought-train of 'there isn't enough time for this, because I need my kids to do well on tests.' Overall, testing is undermining what education is supposed to be doing.

Now, let's stop the ranting and go to the positives of today's middle school learning.

The first thing McTighe discussed was that there is a growing recognition of the harmful effects of the 'standardized testing frenzy'. He remarked how he sees that there is a growing concern, specifically from parents, about testing, with the growing opt-out movement, and then with politicians then getting involved in these well-intended 'power moves'. He said how lots of public money goes towards this fight with testing, and that the idea of having measures of success, like business margins, can be representative of schools. But we know see how the problem with this logic is that education is so much more complex with schools, and how we need more than one 'snapshot' via standardized tests for our 'businesses.' We need changes, and many recognize that – what those are, are not definitive.

After this, McTighe proceeded to bring up the idea of charter school opportunities. Charter schools, for those of you that don't know (I didn't) are schools that are part of the public school system (meaning they obtain funding from the state) and, where if they can get a license to operate, they can start a school with different parameters than public schools. There are many in cities, specifically New York City, and only a few in other areas (due to population densities). These schools, he elaborates, can set up a unique education program, different than what I had talked about this entire book. As an example, McTighe brought up his daughter Maria, who had taught at the High Tech High charter school in San Diego. This school's main focus was project-based learning (something I fully support) where rather than sitting in class for 45 minutes and moving on, school is based around kids learning with authentic projects. This included one which his daughter had worked on, where students and their teacher had to research design and construction of a 'tiny house', an environmentally-friendly self-sustaining house to be erected in a park in San Diego, where the whole project and that school year was planned backward from reaching that goal. Here, the students were able to learn research skills, basic design and engineering (with blueprints and construction), science (with energy efficiency), learn environmental laws and building codes and work around them, finance (budgeting / making money to build the structure), and finally, they actually had to make the project (with the whole process was documented).

What a prime example of how different this type of program is compared to typical schools! Charter schools allow more freedom, and allow for more exciting opportunities. Now yes, there are many successes and failures with these types of programs, but you do have to admit: the potential to get outside the box, to see something alternative like this in middle schools, has the potential to be great!

Now, McTighe also brought up how he shows great support towards project based learning, and also STEM (science, technology, engineering, and math) learning more involved in schools, in order to make learning more hands on, and to give authentic based problem solving practice problems, as opposed to book learning.

Overall, there are some movements that McTighe feels gives him hope in the education system; however, there are still many changes we need to make in education today for the betterment of middle schools.

David Warlick

When asked about his beliefs in regards to the totality of education, David Warlick remarked wrote that,

"What's killing education in America today is high-stakes testing. Albert Einstein is often credited with the following quote, but it should actually be attributed to the Sociologist, William Bruce Cameron.

Not everything that can be counted, counts.

Not everything that counts can be counted.

Every educator will agree with this statement. However, when so much importance it placed on government testing, then education leaders are going to insist that teachers teach what can be measured and in such a way that the measurement reflects well on the school. So we emphasize facts at the expense of understanding. It has damaged our children's education and demoralized the teaching profession.

Before I graduated from college, I spent a year working in a chainsaw factory. For a time, I worked as a quality control engineer, which meant that I used precision instruments to measure motor parts before assembly to assure that they all complied with the blueprint specification, making sure that they were all exactly the same.

This is what we are doing in our schools today. Making sure that all students know the same things, think the same way, and can solve the same problems. This was fine in the industrial age where you needed a workforce who knew the same things and thought the same way.

But today, in a time of rapid change, it is not what you know that's the same as everyone else that brings value to an endeavor. It's what you know that different. How you think that's different. It's your ability to solve new problems that is of value.

There is certainly common knowledge that we should all have. But just as critical is developing and celebrating our differences.

What frightens me the most is that today, almost 20 years after the passage of *No Child Left Behind*, more than half of all teacher in the U.S. have never worked in classrooms where they could be truly creative in their teaching.

CHAPTER **12**

Student Pieces

In order to ensure that you wouldn't be left off with just mainly my writing style, I decided to spice it up a bit and allow some of my peers to assist in getting their ideas across. The following are all un-edited pieces from my fellow classmates.

Chloe Van Dorn

Middle school didn't teach me a few important things. As a freshman in high school, I was shocked by my lack of knowledge about studying properly, especially for cumulative exams. I also wish I had learned a lot more about robotics and computer programming.

In middle school, I was never told how hard high school would be. The tests in middle school were very easy and didn't require much studying or effort. I was so unprepared for the first few tests in high school because they were very difficult and so different from what I was used to. The rigorous honors courses I enrolled in forced me to spend hours studying for tests. This was a change that I was not expecting, as I had never needed to study for tests in years prior. There was also never any homework in middle school, so spending an hour or more a night on homework in high school was an unwelcome surprise. Additionally, midterms and final exams were not given in middle school so when January of freshman year came around, I had no idea how or what to study for the important cumulative exams. Middle schools should be teaching students tips and strategies for doing well on midterms and finals, and even administering cumulative tests in preparation for the real ones that are a big determining factor of final grades in high school.

I am also very interested in technology and robotics. I am currently in the Syosset High School Robotics Club. I wish my middle school had more Computer Science and Robotics courses available to take. The computer classes in middle school were geared towards typing skills and how to use different programs, like Microsoft Word and PowerPoint, not computer programming. I am now very interested in learning how to program robots and make apps and websites. If I had learned that in middle school, I would be a much better programmer in high school. Furthermore, the technology classes in middle school were mostly geared towards woodworking and other simple projects. I enjoy robotics and building bigger things that move. In high school I have had to work very hard to learn how to build with the pieces and to learn what everything does. If I had begun learning how to build robots in middle school, everything would have been so much easier for me when I joined the club in ninth grade. The students in high school who already know about robotics from outside organizations in middle school are already more successful in the Robotics Club because of their experience. If all freshmen could come into the high school with a basic knowledge of robotics, our team would do really well in the competitions. I am now the Vice President of the Robotics Club. I worked very hard to earn this prestigious position and if I had learned about robotics when I was younger, I could be doing even more to help lead our team to victory. Robotics and computer programming teach children how to problem solve and create their own designs. I strongly believe that kids should be educated about these important classes in middle school.

Overall, I really enjoyed my experience in middle school. If I had learned a little more about what studying in high school is really like and about robotics and technology, I might have had an easier time in ninth grade. Otherwise, I had a lot of fun in middle school and I learned a lot!

Emilee Meltzer

Middle school is such an important year for everyone, as it is the bridge between childhood and adolescence. Looking back on my middle school years I think what I learned could have been enhanced. For example, in social studies, we mainly only learn about the things that happened many years ago. I think it is very important to engulf the students in current events that are happening everyday. Society changes daily and it is so important for developing adults to understand the rights and wrongs of the events occurring everyday. Unfortunately this does not happen and continues to be neglected.

Also, the common core that has been put into action has only been hurting students. The students in my grade were fortunate to still be taught the traditional way of learning. For the younger kids, learning is no longer something that is looked forward to. My brother is in 7th grade and he is probably more stressed out than I am. The way he is learning is so complicated he cannot explain it to anyone else because he barely understands it himself. Going to school should be about truly understanding a topic and being excited to learn about new things. Now, education has taught students how to memorize, cheat, and sulk starting at very young ages, which I feel is extremely dangerous.

In middle school, I also wish that I had learned how to truly speak Spanish. Although I have taken Spanish since the 3rd grade, I still cannot have a conversation and fully comprehend what the other person is saying. The foundation of anything new is extremely important as it molds the way the final product is going to turn out. The foundation of the language I have been learning consisted of learning new vocabulary and taking a test on it, which did nothing besides hurt me in the long run. I just wish we learned more about how to hold a real conversation in the language we took in middle school. Looking back, I learned many things that have been so influential throughout high school so far. I just feel as if middle school can be changed to be even more impactful than it is right now starting with tweaking the way information is being taught.

Jake Gould

Middle school opened my eyes. When entering middle school, everyone seemed so innocent. Nobody had any intention of doing anything hurtful to others, everyone always felt wanted. After entering middle school, this soon changed. People changed. Friends changed. Some for the better, but some for the worse. Because this happened so abruptly, it felt like a smack in the face. I don't think middle school prepared us for this change. How am I supposed to deal with dropping friends because they have turned into people I don't want to associate myself with. Friends who no longer seem to share my same interests because they are trying to grow up so quickly. Some already experimenting with alcohol and drugs. Many of these kids I have known with since preschool, now it seems we are just on different paths.

When it comes to academics, middle school should be more focused on not only preparing us for high school, but also preparing us for our future. As someone who has always been fascinated with business, why am I forced to take gym everyday? I ran track and played tennis after school. Instead of gym, an introduction to accounting class should be offered. Sewing and cooking class may be helpful to some students, however; many students would probably benefit from choosing an elective of their choice. Although high school offers electives that are more diverse, I don't see any reason as to why middle school cannot offer more electives that would help guide us into paths so we know whether or not we like something by the time we enter high school.

Is standardized testing too much? I do not think so. I think the idea of all students throughout New York State taking uniform tests is a great idea. This way, we can see which schools need to improve and which schools the state needs to support more academically. By having these common tests, students are better able to gauge their academic progress.

Jarrad Li

There is a whole lot that South Woods Middle School didn't teach me. But I'm not saying South Woods is faulty for not teaching me these things. Most middle schools don't teach these things at all. One thing South Woods didn't teach me is how to perform regular life tasks. Yes, I know, parents are supposed to teach these things. But shouldn't schools go over how to perform life chores? I don't know, maybe elementary schools should. Middle school didn't teach me how to wash dishes, use a vacuum cleaner, do the laundry, etc. Middle school never taught me how to manage money or any basic financial skills. I know schools are supposed to educate you to be successful in life, but financial skills are obviously required to be successful in life. Financial decision-making is an important skill middle schools don't teach. Middle school never taught me how to program. Digital skills, in a world growing more technological every day, are crucial in life success. Using different types of new popular technology should be in the middle school curriculums. Programming is also necessary in many different careers. Speaking of careers, middle schools don't teach courses that allow students to effectively pursue a career of interest. They skim over this topic as if it isn't necessary, which it obviously is. Students need to find a career of interest and pursue it throughout high school. Middle school never taught students about relationships. Relationship counseling should be important in all schools. Kids need to learn about relationships more effectively in order to achieve a healthy social life. Middle schools also never taught kids about wordplay. Debate is an important aspect of most careers, and negotiation skills are vital in a successful life. Middle school never taught me how important failing is. Nobody achieves success without any failure. If middle schools would have taught us that if we don't struggle, we don't get any better, we would be much better at problem solving in general. Although middle school had family consumer science classes, these classes never taught me how to perform basic cooking tasks. I never learned how to cook using the stove, fry an egg, or use the dishwasher. Basic survival skills such as swimming, finding water when stranded, using a first aid kit, and fixing a leak, are completely ignored by middle schools in their curriculum. Middle schools also skim over time management, an important life skill. Is there a reason why so many kids nowadays procrastinate or have no time completing homework or projects? Yes, because school doesn't teach us priorities. If someone has to study for a test but has too much homework, he or she should know to B.S. some of the homework and look at them later to go study for the test, which is obviously more important, but schools don't teach us that. Instead of having band or orchestra, which are utterly useless, middle school should teach kids how to get better at their instrument individually instead of playing useless easy music together. Math classes only look at a distinct way to solve problems. Creative problem solving is a valuable skill in life. Not all the steps of the "middle school way" of solving problems are necessary, and sometimes these steps get you nowhere in solving difficult or creative problems. Different and unique approaches to problems should be looked at. History classes in middle school have a biased worldview, in general. They only look at the European or American point of view when regarding world events. They never look through, let's say, the African point of view. Middle school didn't teach me the power of being unique. A student must stand out from everyone else in order to be accepted into a good college or for a job. The power of innovation is also skipped over by middle schools. Creations such as Facebook or the first handheld phone win people millions or even billions of dollars. Innovation is what drives human beings to be what they are now, superior to all other organisms. The curriculum skims over European fallacies or mistakes, but it emphasizes European successes and achievements. Also, middle school didn't teach me how valuable life actually is. I have been living life as if I deserve time on this Earth, which is completely wrong. People suffer and people die every day. To have such a luxurious life is considered lucky by most of the people in this world. Finally, and most importantly, middle school didn't teach me how to hit the Quan.

That is the most important skill in life, and I don't know where humanity would be without knowing how to hit the Quan.

Kenneth Chou

Middle school was a place for development in many immature children. It was a place where children learned to develop their skills academically and socially. In middle school, everyone wanted to be classified as "cool", but unfortunately, not everyone could achieve that "level" of popularity. Children were always nagging their parents about getting the clothes, shoes, socks, or backpacks of the newest trend, just trying to "fit in". Apparently, being cool meant cursing, being popular on social media, and playing sports. But what middle school should've taught students is that trying to be someone that you aren't is fake and not beneficial for the future.

Overall, middle school did not teach children how to be themselves. Middle school also didn't teach students how to succeed in a high school course. The leap from 8th grade in middle school to 9th grade in high school was unnecessarily big in the workload. Eighth grade classes did not require a huge amount of work and effort, but as high school approached, courses like biology, geometry, and world history occupied great amounts of time, stunning students and overloading them with work. Eighth grade classes were very relaxed, and most of the classes did not count towards the college transcript, so students did not stress over the class. Therefore students had to adapt to staying up later, managing their time, and working hard in high school. Middle school also did not emphasize the importance of guidance counselors, and how helpful and supportive they could be. Middle school didn't show students that guidance counselors are always willing to do what's best for the students. All in all, middle school shaped many students into who they are today, but did not emphasize many aspects of school life.

Sammi Landsman

Middle school prepared me very well for high school, but lacked in teaching me two main components of high school education. Note taking is one of the most important skills to master throughout high school, yet I had no idea how to take notes when I started AP world social studies. I figured it out easily, but it was obvious that other students were not prepared to take the type of notes we were required to take.

Another major factor the middle school education system left out was challenging questions, the questions in middle school were either regents level or below, especially in science, but in high school science, we jumped to SAT 2 subject test questions that were extremely difficult, there was no transition and the questions were difficult to understand, but with enough exposure, became easier, these two factors of high school are extremely important and should be taken into more consideration in the middle school curriculum.

CHAPTER 13

Conclusion

Now, with the entirety of my ideas and beliefs, as well as those of a multitude of others, bestowed upon you, I would like to discuss the ways in which we can actually go about making these changes.

Students, anywhere from Kindergarten to High School, can actually do more than they think in regards to making change.

Firstly, I think that all students should constantly be reflecting on themselves with one question: "What more do I need to succeed?"

It's a simple question, but an extremely important one, as there is always something more that students can learn or practice. After all, even the best educational curriculums can't teach students everything they need to know. Once students can understand what they need, they can make their own way on a variety of educational paths. They can either learn it themselves, or take the better long-term path: to try to make a change.

Parents of these students also can do a lot to help understand what needs to be done in the education system. Often times, and I know it's been the case with me, parents will know their children almost as well as the kids know themselves. As such, parents should be able to understand how a student may be performing in a certain topic, but also should be able to notice how they go about their everyday life and what they do. After taking stock of what some of these kids don't know, they can come up with a strong list of what they feel the students aren't being taught or aren't being taught in the best way.

Now, here comes the important part: implementing change with members of the school board and politicians, in order to make proactive changes to our education system. The only way to get this type of education-reform success, for the most part, is in-house, or in-district. Thus, in this scenario, school board members hold the cards. And honestly, there is a lot that you can do.

First off, you can always go to a board meeting. Here you can observe the current curriculum, as well as partake in the 'audience to the public' section of the meeting. Additionally, I encourage anyone and everyone who is willing and dedicated to get on their town's respective curriculum committee, or whatever your district has that is similar. Many times, this is through the PTSA, and participating in these types of committees can help accomplish much.

Likewise, anyone can start and follow through with a petition to the district's administration, where, if enough support is gained, you might be able to make real change quickly and effectively. Further, anyone is capable of lobbying your own state government to make new legislation.

Now, these are just a handful of actions that anybody can partake in to see real change. There are many more routes to take, but I hope these representatives show you as to what anyone can do with education curriculum change.

Finally, one thing is important to remember with these types of changes: change won't happen overnight. My brother, Josh, at 18 years old, ran for the School Board of our town, won, has been on for the past 4 years, and still finds difficulty in making quick changes. He actually wrote a book on it, and about young people could run for office, entitled Political Gladiators. It's a good read; I encourage you to buy a copy.

It will take consistent effort from teachers, parents, students, and politicians alike to bring about the necessary changes. So, get out there and make a difference!

With everything said and done, go out, explore the world.

Thanks for reading!

About the Experts

Many of the experts I had the pleasure of interviewing are so incredibly in their respective fields, and I am so lucky that I had the ability to interview each and every one of them.

Alan Kay

Alan Kay is a computer scientist, who has been elected a Fellow of the American Academy of Arts and Sciences, the National Academy of Engineering, and the Royal Society of Arts. He revolutionized computer science with his incredible work on object oriented programming, and graphical user interface design. Currently, he is the president of the Viewpoints Research Institute, and is an Adjunct Professor at UCLA.

Alan November

Alan November is an international leader in education technology, with a heavy background in education. He has been a teacher, a director of an alternative high school, computer coordinator, technology consultant, and university lecturer. Currently, through his company November Learning, he helps schools, governments, and industry leaders improve the quality of education through technology.

Andy Hunt

Andy Hunt co-authored the famous book The Pragmatic Programmer, as well as six other software development books and many articles. He was also one of the 17 original authors of the Agile Manifesto and founders of the Agile Alliance.

Bill Ayers

Bill Ayers is a retired and distinguished professor of education at the University of Illinois at Chicago, formerly holding the title of Distinguished Professor of Education and Senior University Scholar. Now, Ayers is an American elementary education theorist, among many other pursuits in the field of education.

Bjarne Stroustrup

Bjarne Stroustrup is a computer scientist, who also is the creator of the widely used C++ programming language. He is a Distinguished Research Professor, currently holding the College of Engineering Chair at Texas A&M University. He is the recipient of the Grace Murray Hopper Award, an award given to computer scientists who have made significant contributions to the computer science society before the age of 35. Additionally, he is a visiting professor at Columbia University, and works in New York as a Managing Director for Morgan Stanley.

Brian Kernighan

Brian Kernighan is a computer scientist, who also helped develop the Unix operating system, the gateway to future operating systems and a major breakthrough in computer programming. He also helped play a role in the AWK and AMPL programming languages, and co-wrote the first ever book about the C programming language. Since 2000, Kernighan has been a Professor at the Computer Science Department at Princeton University.

David Warlick

David Warlick is an educator, author, programmer, and public speaker. As an early adopter and advocate for technology in the classroom for more than 30 years, Warlick has taught and written about technology integration and education. Also, in 2011, Technology & Learning Magazine named Warlick one of the Ten Most Influential People in EdTech.

Deborah Meier

Deborah Meier is often considered the founder of the modern 'small schools movement', ranking among the most acclaimed leaders of education reform in the US. Meier has done everything in education, from being a kindergarten teacher to founding and directing of an alternative school. In 2009, the National Center for Fair and Open Testing named an annual award after Meier, entitled the "Deborah W. Meier Hero in Education Award".

Doug Reeves

Doug Reeves is a nationally known education author and provider of professional development for school leaders, writing over 20 books, and has received some of the most noteworthy awards in the field of education reform. Reeves is the founder of The Leadership and Learning Center, an international organization dedicated to improving student achievement and educational equity.

Guido Van Rossum

Guido van Rossum is a computer scientist who is best known for creating the Python programming language, and is arguably the most important coder of our generation. Van Rossum has worked at top companies, such as Google and Dropbox, his current place of employment. He authored and co-authored dozens of books and articles on Python, multimedia, and several other operating systems and programs.

Jay McTighe

Jay McTighe is an experienced educator, noted author, and keynote speaker in the field of education reform. Through his company of Jay McTighe & Associates, McTighe provides consulting services to schools, districts, regional service agencies, and state departments of education.

Matt Krisiloff

Matt Krisiloff is best known as one of the managers of Y Combinator Fellowship at Y Combinator, a prominent venture capital firm in the US. This program involves the allotment of equity free loans to idea-stage startups in the country. Prior, he worked at Hyde Park Angels, one of the Midwest's largest angel organizations.

Paul Graham

Paul Graham is a programmer, writer, and investor. In 2005, he started Y Combinator, the first of a new type of startup incubator, where, since 2005, Y Combinator has funded over 800 startups, including Dropbox, Airbnb, Stripe, and Reddit. He is also known for his famous essays on entrepreneurship, programming, and on life in general, was the original founder of the predecessor to Yahoo Store, and is known for his incredible work with the LISP programming language.

Robert Goodman

Robert Goodman is the Executive Director for the New Jersey Center for Teaching and Learning, an organization whose mission is to empower teachers to be leaders in the transformation of public schools so that all students have access to a high quality education. Goodman was also the 2006 New Jersey Teacher of the Year, prior to the start of the NJCTL.

Robert Marzano

Robert Marzano is a premier educational speaker, trainer, writer, and overall expert in the United States. His work has been published in over 30 books and 150 publications, on tipics including instruction, assessment, writing and implementing standards, and effective leadership. His practical translations of the most current research and theory into classroom strategies are internationally known and widely practiced by both teachers and administrators.

Terri Sjodin

Terri Sjodin is the principal and founder of Sjodin Communications, a prominent public speaking, sales training and consulting firm. She is one of America's most highly sought after female speakers and has trained and motivated thousands of people from all over the world. Sjodin is also a bestselling author, writing Small Message, Big Impact.

Thomas Cormen

Thomas H. Cormen is a computer scientist best known for his work with algorithms. He is the co-author of Introduction to Algorithms, as well as the newer book Algorithms Unlocked. In addition, he is a full professor of computer science at Dartmouth College, and currently is chairing the department as well.

Ward Cunningham

Ward Cunningham is a computer programmer, who is best known for his work in developing the first Wiki (think: Wikipedia). He is also a pioneer in both design patterns and extreme programming, and has authored books regarding his development of the first wiki. Currently, he is a software engineer at New Relic.

Final List of Those Students Who Helped

Below are all of the students who helped me either through over-the-phone interviews to obtain an understanding of my peers' beliefs or those who assisted by writing a one-page piece for the book. Thanks to you all.

Alvee Chowdhury
Chloe Van Dorn
Emilee Meltzer
Jake Gould
Jarrad Li
Jeremy Weiss
Jon DiSiena
Kenneth Chou
Michael Stanco
Nishant Bhaumik
Sabrina Kagan
Scott Haft

ABOUT THE AUTHOR

Aaron Lafazan is the type of guy who'd rather build towers out of Red Solo Cups than read a book. He is a 15-year-old student at Syosset High School on Long Island, New York, where he currently maintains a 98.5 average. Prior to writing the book, Aaron was an avid burrito eater and Netflix watcher. When not listening to Ashkan Moghaddassi's Soundcloud, he is most likely utilizing one of his specialty talents, which include late night movie selection, making websites, and movie quoting. After moving once during his lifetime (down the street by two miles), Aaron currently resides in his hometown of Syosset, where he lives with his mother Sandy, his father Jeffrey, and Josh and Justin, and his two brothers.